MYSTIC LIVING

The principles of Vaastu
for the 21st century

Raymond Prohs

First published by O Books, 2007
O Books is an imprint of John Hunt Publishing Ltd.,
The Bothy, Deershot Lodge, Park Lane, Ropley, Hants, SO24 0BE, UK
office1@o-books.net
www.o-books.net

Distribution in:

UK and Europe
Orca Book Services
orders@orcabookservices.co.uk
Tel: 01202 665432 Fax: 01202 666219 Int. code (44)

USA and Canada
NBN
custserv@nbnbooks.com
Tel: 1 800 462 6420 Fax: 1 800 338 4550

Australia and New Zealand
Brumby Books
sales@brumbybooks.com.au
Tel: 61 3 9761 5535 Fax: 61 3 9761 7095

Far East (offices in Singapore, Thailand, Hong Kong, Taiwan)
Pansing Distribution Pte Ltd
kemal@pansing.com
Tel: 65 6319 9939 Fax: 65 6462 5761

South Africa
Alternative Books
altbook@peterhyde.co.za
Tel: 021 447 5300 Fax: 021 447 1430

Text copyright Raymond Prohs 2007

Design: Stuart Davies

ISBN: 978 1 905047 98 7

A CIP catalogue record for this book is available from the British Library.

Printed in the US by Maple Vail

MYSTIC LIVING

The principles of Vaastu
for the 21st century

Raymond Prohs

BOOKS

Winchester, UK
Washington, USA

To my mother and father, Genevieve and Gardner...and to the Divine Lineage of masters and the gifts their wisdom is manifesting in our lives...now, at the turn of the Age.

ACKNOWLEDGEMENTS

To all those who have, in one way or another, helped me see my way to writing this book: Daniela, Ramakrishna, Monika & Gary, Nityaananda, Brett, Paul, Johanna, Nancy, Berta, Myuri, Christinea, and Eric...my heartful thanks. My gratitude also goes to John Hunt and everyone at O Books, who have bound my thoughts and words in so tangible a form. And, to Sri Sai Kaleshwara Swami, who has made everything mystical a practical, living reality for so many of us.

CONTENTS

PREFACE

SPIRITUALITY & THE JOYS OF HANGING BY A THREAD

MAKE A MENTAL, HEARTFUL & SOULFUL NOTE: Vaastu is 50% of spirituality. That's a golden statement. Whether you're consciously on a spiritual path or not, your relationship with your environment is *the* single most important ingredient in your life. We can argue 'consciousness' or, if you like, 'the Divine', but how many know exactly how conscious they are? How many know the yardstick to measure by? We live in the world, cross-referenced with our inner world(s). And, it is our relationship with everything that lives, breathes, laughs, and grows, or sits, turns, gravitates, or goes farther than the eye can see — outward or inward, visible and invisible — all this, we call 'life'. This is the environment we live in. And, it is the environment through which we move along the path of our soul. Since, in any discussion, we have to start somewhere, let's start this one in the best place possible — our own backyard.

In 1985, my mother died of cancer. For 20 years she lived in a house with the front door facing the southwest of our property; the house also had an east-southeast entrance through our garage, which we all used every day; and she faced south when cooking our meals. At the time, like most Westerners, I wouldn't have made a connection between my mother's illness and any 'home features'. The best guess of the five doctors that took care of her in the end was that the sad, confusing, singular 'probable' cause of her death was second-hand smoke. Yet, not long after, I learned some things I'm sure her doctors never considered. According to manuscripts written over 5,000 years ago, entrances in the southwest and east-southeast and facing south while cooking (using fire) are life-threatening 'defects' — particularly for women.

My first introduction to Vaastu came during my second trip to India. I went to source high-quality, wild-crafted herbs for my Ayurvedic practice back in the US. At one stop, I was invited by the owner of a 'natural' pharmacy to stay a day or two in his home — a beautiful sprawling compound with gardens and a man-made pond fed from a 20-foot-high fountain. The rooms in his magnificent home were bathed in natural light streaming in through windows facing east; the floors were tiered — both upstairs and down; the rooms in the south were higher than the rooms in the north and east, if only by a few inches. I commented on the 'unique' plan of the house and property and was told it was all built according to Vaastu. In fact, all their properties were. Moreover, this man was sure Vaastu was the foundation of his and his family's success and good health. He took me to his office and showed me a 'book' on Vaastu made of palm leaves. It was his family's 'bible for building'.

They had always been wealthy, as far as he knew, and long-lived (in India, where they keep records that are literally thousands of years old, that's saying something). And, the one constancy in their family tradition was that they always built according to Vaastu. The richest family in a valley known for its wealthy inhabitants, this current generation had founded three universities (two technical, one medical), two hospitals, an Ayurvedic pharmacy, and an allopathic one. There were four generations living in near proximity and every piece of property — and every structure on those properties — was built according to Vaastu.

His arguments were articulate, his enthusiasm endearing, but my still predominantly Western mind thought, "It's just circumstantial." Patiently, compassionately — he clearly picked up on my skepticism — he offered a short-form history of Vaastu. The ancient maharishis ('great seers') — men and women of extraordinary insight and miraculous spiritual power — passed on their wisdom in texts, which they called the Vedas. One aspect of the Vedas, the science of Vaastu, deals specifically with the influences of the cosmic forces in nature on the quality of life of the inhabitants of a particular place. It was the first 'natural' science of architecture, pre-dating Feng Shui by more than 3,000 years.

In Inda, it is said that Vaastu and Feng Shui are like grandfather and grandson. Thousands of years ago a powerful Bengali prince begged a wandering mendicant to heal his dying wife. That man, a saint from China, agreed, and soon the princess recovered. The prince offered the holy man anything he wished, up to half the prince's kingdom. The sage replied, "I want your library." It is said he returned to China with over 6,500 volumes of Vedic texts — many on Vaastu.

The wisdom of the maharishis came in the form of *shruti* and *shmriti* — divinely revealed knowledge, and observation and practical application of their direct inner experiences. Through their meditation practices, the ancient sages realized the existence of underlying forces whose source and expressions could be known through personal experience, even though they were not apparent in the world of the senses. These 'invisible' cosmic forces (and entities) the maharishis called 'the Divine'. How to contact them, how to build a personal, soulful, and permanent relationship with them was first revealed to the seers by angels — energetic 'intelligences', which imparted the sacred formulas for spiritual enlightenment.

Applying this 'spiritual' knowledge in the world of solid appearances was accomplished first by observation. Then, they tested all angles. For example, to increase and hold the *shakti* (spiritual power) of meditation they found greater results meditating in nature, where the energy was more peaceful; by doing it with water to the north, northeast, and/or east and having the northeast open and uncluttered, the divine energy flowed more easily; having a mountain behind them to the south, southwest, and west protected their processes from the disruptive energy that naturally flowed from that direction. Through their observations, testings, and direct experience they came to understand how the Divine played in the world. Understanding Vaastu became a practical way to predict and positively influence life events.

The fundamental cosmic forces or 'Pillars of Creation', as the maharishis described them, were given the name, *panchabhutas,* the Five Elements: earth, fire, sky (*akasha*/ether/space), water, and air. Each has its own characteristics, its own qualities. Based on their 'placement' — where and how they are situated on the property and in the home — they exert either good or bad influences on the inhabitants. Too much height and weight (the Earth element) in the north, for example, makes holding onto and accumulating wealth nearly impossible and, furthermore, is an extreme life-risk.

These 'elements' are energies or forces in nature, which strongly influence the physical, emotional, and mental world(s) we each live in — forces that work in specific ways and produce specific results. Each of the Five Elements has directional strengths and exerts either positive or negative influences based on their placement. According to the Great Seers, if we live in accord with these natural forces, the majority of our problems — the majority of all mankind's problems — are solved. Their testings proved that creating a sacred space in accord with the laws of nature was the most solid foundation for creating a beautiful, powerful, successful, healthy and happy life and, certainly, a must for a spiritual one.

Naturally, I wanted more 'modern' proof. That's how the story of my mother's death in the context of her life became a case in point. Over the following months, as I read any book I could find on Vaastu and tracked my life according to the residences I lived in — in the configurations of rooms, entrances, street access, and property angles — I realized my life was my proof.

However, Vaastu's main strength isn't just in its ability to show where we've been or where we're going if we remain in the home (and/or workplaces) we're in. More importantly, it also shows how to use the divine energetics of nature to structure real change in our 'real' world. According to the maharishis, the majority of our karma is changeable through Vaastu. Change your Vaastu and you change your life. That, too, is a golden statement.

Before students came to my Master's ashram, Sri Sai Kaleshwara lived in a hut there, in what was then a dense, centuries-old forest butting up against an imposing mountain. Over the years, from the days of the hut to today, the nature in the ashram has been sculpted according to Vaastu principles. With each change — moving tons of dirt, expanding northeast and east, raising walls, building new structures, on and on — he tested the energy through its significance on his own spiritual processes and through the results evident in those of the growing student population. But, from the start, he followed Vaastu: the hut itself, where he spent most of his time, either inside or at the *dhuni* (fire pit) nearby, is a perfect Vaastu structure. Excellent Vaastu is not dependent on external grandeur. Nature is everywhere. Whether you live in a palace or a hut, the immense harmony of nature can be harnessed through following the guidelines of Vaastu.

Through his personal testings and study of the ancient texts and consultations with modern Vaastu experts, he found many invaluable distinctions between what he came to know from his own study and personal experience and the general modern presentation of Vaastu. One, which is of enormous importance because of its vast applications, is the singular value traditionalists place on the east. It is commonly given greatest importance because it carries the energetics of wisdom; and, of course, the east is associated with the broad dynamics of the Sun's energy, with its early morning healing power and the recognized spiritual and material values of its light. But, in his testings it was made clear that the energetics of the north was equally important for it carries the energetics of abundance/wealth, and that highest importance should actually go to the convergence of the two, to the northeast. From the northeast come the highest divine energies — the full mixing of abundance and wisdom. When a property (or building) is extended in that direction, it is a great boon to the inhabitants in numerous ways. Here's the point: it is a characteristic of our times, this *Kaliyuga* or Dark Age, that wealth, especially, (yet, wisdom as well) comes and goes easily. It is the nature, the common experience. Wealth not only helps fulfill basic physical needs and facilitates material comforts. In this Age, when spirituality is very much about suburban centers, international retreats, and gathering community, as well as converging solitude, service and personal growth in the midst of broadening bandwidth, cross-border conflicts and cultural contrasts, ease of access is a daily requirement and challenge. In such a world, wealth helps. And so, it is a valuable ingredient in one's spirituality. It's a challenge this Age presents us head-on: to possess wealth, with little or no attachment, and use it for spiritual upliftment, for ourselves and for as many others as we possibly can.

THE CHALLENGE OF THIS AGE

It is a known, yet strangely unappreciated truth: spiritual laws change over time. Too often, we give an absolute value to authoritative texts, whether they are spiritual (or supernatural) in origin or academic. On top of that, we rely almost entirely on what is publicly accessible or at least commonly recognized. In this light, it's got to be clear that some things…some *important* things…might probably have slipped through the cracks. One such important thing is that spiritual laws change over time. These days, this point is considered off-handedly, even dismissed as anomalous. Why? One part, it's because the dynamics and inner mechanics are misunderstood (or go unrecognized by-and-large), especially by those whose 'expertise' is founded almost entirely on book-learning, as well-read as they may be. It's simply easier and more convenient to give an absolute status to 'the Word' and allow the, well, plethora of anomalies to remain exalted in their status as esoterica, 'spiritual mysteries'. However, the dynamics of nature are not confined solely to the realms of theory, conjecture, opinion, or mystery. That is why every branch of knowledge (including our modern sciences) has an arm, which attempts to practically apply that knowledge in nature — not merely to prove or disprove the theory, but to understand and utilize its parameters *in nature*. This is equally true (in fact, more so) when it comes to the spiritual arts and sciences. It takes a spiritual artist/scientist with direct experience of the underlying dynamics of nature, who possesses a deep, discriminating understanding of those dynamics and their applications, to apply them successfully.

Vaastu is not just about beautiful pastel colors and sari-covered walls or spiritually evocative embellishments (remember the hut); it is foremost about understanding the forces of nature and harnessing its harmonious energies for the benefit of the inhabitants. Its modern resurgence is a boon to our generation.

The presentation of this most-modern understanding of Vaastu is not to undermine those who've been moved by the knowledge and inspiration of traditional Vaastu or Feng Shui or other forms of 'natural' architecture. Nor is this meant to cause fear, only perhaps a reasonable amount of common sense (a wholly spiritual attribute) and heartful discrimination. There are those who've come to these systems via lively conversation, cocktail talk or classes on floral arrangements and modern landscape design, even courses on Eastern philosophy, and/or by recognizing the growing tide of interest and the real possibility of etching out a niche in the marketplace. Certainly, these too have a place in our multi-faceted world. But...or and...my advice on such a beautiful and vast subject: come to some personal understanding, study and test it (as much as you can), *own it*...then follow whatever clarity is in your heart. At the very least, you'll come to some informed decisions on which experts to follow; at most, you'll change your life for the better...forever.

So, what is the challenge of this Age? While absolutism-for-convenience-sake touches much of spirituality, it is more of a distraction than a challenge. In truth, it is simply an unfortunate misinterpretation, which can easily and readily be righted. There are billions of people; and so...literally...there are billions of spiritual paths to walk, one for each of us. No one walks the same path in the same way as anyone else. However, there are certain doors in common, which we each must walk through sooner or later. Again, that's a spiritual law. For true spiritual Realization — or, gaining a Ph.D. in Spirituality, as my Master calls it — we must gain a commanding on the natural (supernatural) forces. And, whether your system calls them the Five Elements or not, we each have to reach that plateau for true spiritual success. Part of that process is washing (giving up) our blocks — our personal sense of unworthiness, jealousy, greed, etc. Another part is increasing our soul capacity so we can hold the divine energy. For this, we do *sadhana* (spiritual practices: japa, meditation, whatever it is). Together, these increase our capacity to love with an open heart...and love impels everything else: our competence, skill, the capacity to connect and share the joys of life, and to relieve the heartbreak and hardships that others are burdened with. Even to heal them, through the Divine's grace.

Of course, each of these is a treatise in itself. But, you and I have the present, sweet luxury of this being only an introduction to this wisdom, not the full breadth and depth of it. In an ancient, wonderful book called *The Yogavasistha*, Guru Vasistha (Lord Rama's family guru) has an enlightening conversation with his divine student, which it is said lasted 9 days. The 'transcript' of that conversation is the second longest book ever written. In reading a very beautifully adapted (and extremely abridged) version, I was deeply touched by many of the sublime points, and one in particular: at one point the guru says, "The highest wisdom seeks you out of its own accord." Such an amazing thing to say! It is the wisdom that seeks you out when the time is ripe — when you are ripe. For those who wish to dive deeply into the ocean of this knowledge, the path is open...*welcome!* My Master is fond of saying we are all in the same boat. It is the Master's duty to throw us in the water. It is our duty to swim around, plumb some depths, get to know the currents, become familiar with them, master them, and share that mastery with others. But, we should always know: there is a thread tied between us — Master and student — so that we will successfully win our passage. For those who wish a beautiful life for themselves, their families, friends, and co-workers, you too will find substantive, practical miracles here. Study them, test them, and apply them to your life. You'll see a huge difference. Change your Vaastu and you change your life...it's a spiritual law.

INTRODUCTION

LIVING BEYOND YOUR MEANS BUT NOT YOUR CAPACITY

How do we judge what is real, what is true? Mostly, we gauge it by what others ('experts') say, balanced with what we personally perceive and, in turn, are willing to accept. Isn't this true? Mom says something is true; we believe her (in her), so we believe that what she says is also true. We consider the source first and accept the knowledge/info as wise/true based upon our personal perception, which includes our direct knowledge and our personal cluster of beliefs. In the process of growing up, we soon (relatively soon, anyway) come to recognize that the 'sources' of knowledge we've accepted are fallible — worst-case scenario, 'fallible,' here, meaning 'wrong'. So, now, at the beginning of a new millennium, at the turn of a new Age, we in the West find ourselves coming to acknowledge — and accept — that even with our cultural bias for 'objectivity', *subjectivity* underlies everything we think and know. We've come to see that the chronicles of history — and history itself — are a rendering, a 'retelling'. In our lifetimes, again and again, it's evident that the warp-and-woof of historical events clearly lies in the personal significance given them by the one (or ones) doing the retelling. As often as not, the so-called proofs given to substantiate the events are prioritized by the needs and wants (and, again, the biases) of the author. Whether they are given merit by personal account or a set of accepted criteria, it's now pretty clear that in the end it comes down to what the author/speaker/teller presents as important. Questioning the 'truth' of the retelling — even dismissing it or, on the contrary, taking it as gospel — is also simply and clearly a matter of personal choice.

"What is the truth…and how do we know it?" are questions that beg answers beyond the realm of academic bibliographies and chronicled circumstances. Just above, I characterized us — you and I — as 'we in the West'. Forgive the pigeon-hole but, ironically, as a group we need singling out in this regard: not just because we have a strong cultural inclination to objectify…everything…and to lend a quasi-absolute character to the role of people, places and things; but because we are just now coming to recognize the lack of real depth and value in this. It is only in the last hundred or so years that we on the whole have embraced forms of 'interior' human sciences, which attempt to plumb the depths of our minds while searching for the meaning of terms such as 'heart' and 'soul'.

Until recently, for better or for worse, our orthodox religions had traditionally remained our 'highest' authority over this domain. But, that is changing too. When it comes to the realm of spirituality — where the salient materials are derived from 'unseen' sources that can't be explained (or explained away) by merely citing places and dates or even social theorem, but are *always* a matter of direct experience — we have begun to turn to the Eastern perspective that *subjectivity* is indeed key. While, as yet, many of us may not fully embrace the ancient Indian, Vedic tenet *'aham brahmasmi'* ('I am everything/everything is Me'), we are, in growing numbers, turning to the proponents of this perspective for their advice and council. Still others of us have turned to living embodiments of this wisdom, to spiritual Masters, for direct guidance — not merely for intellectual understanding or the social ramifications a new and ancient perspective may bring; but to plumb the depths of what lies beyond and within, with the heartful intent of living a mystical life. We as individuals and as a culture are turning a new page.

Mystic living is not something new. Every culture has had its seers and saints. But, one land certainly stands apart in this regard: since the pre-dawn of society/culture itself, through the four Vedic Ages — of *Satyuga*, *Tretayuga*, *Dwarapayuga* and our present *Kaliyuga* — *Bharata*, the land known as India, has retold the stories of living Masters and their teachings. India itself is a sacred power spot, walked upon by thousands of saints, generation after generation, since the dawn of time to this day. It is a beautiful story.

What makes a life mystical is not its mystery. Mystery itself lies in the perspective of those not yet mystical enough. What makes a life mystical lies in the conscious, intimate connection one has with the depth and breadth of Life, what one lives, experiences, recognizes and relates to — from the sacred to the so-called mundane and every level in between.

When we step flat-footed into the realm of Perception and begin to familiarize ourselves with the lay of the land, we find more than we imagined, but not necessarily from the first toe-dunk. It is said that spirituality starts out as poison and ends as *amruta* (divine nectar). The converse is said of the material path: it starts out as nectar and turns to poison. However, those who take the step — and master the spiritual path — leave an indelible mark on everyone and everything they and their story touch. Some of their stories (or parts, anyway) flit now and then through this book. It is their experience, and what I've come to know and experience myself of it, that lies at the heart of Mystic Living.

Within the growing worldwide spiritual community the question is repeated again and again, "How did *they* (the saints) do it?" But, the larger, truly higher, and better question is, "How do *we* do it?" Like so much in life, the inner mechanics of the saints' personal journeys have remained obscured by time, for one, but also very often by design. Secrecy is very important. But, secrecy itself can become a habit that, once it's spread its wings, can and inevitably does become a drawback and a hindrance if it reigns solely to keep others out or worse, to foist 'studentism' instead of nurturing mastery. In the lives of many past and modern-day saints and gurus, this is too often the unfortunate tendency. How many have shared the journals of their personal path — their personal spiritual practices, *mantras, yantras* (sacred symbols), etc.? Certainly not with more than a chosen one or two favored students. More often than not, we know many tidbits of their biographical histories (their origins and travels...many names and places), but what of their inner personal work for Realization? Many gurus in the past, including our personal pasts, did not say, "Here, try this. This is what I've gone through. Let me know if you have any questions. I'm happy to help." No. Again, at least not but to a few disciples, if at all. Today, with so many choices and the greater ease of coming together and sharing Ways and Paths, we can't help but notice some not-so-positive side effects of this practice.

For one, as a result, there arises a seemingly unfordable chasm between Teacher and student regarding personal experiences. All-to-regularly, separate positions are staked out, where the Teacher is God(like) and the student at His/Her feet is minion. In the ancient Vedic tradition (actually, at the heart of every deeply time-tested one), sitting at a Master's feet is an act of love born of respect *based on direct experience*. Direct experience, and the inner 'knowing' that results from it, is the essence of *faith*. Otherwise, it is simply an act of pride on one side and greed (and/or mere 'belief') on the other. The thing of it is, at the depth of it *and* on the surface, a true Master is a friend, a brother, sister. The only real difference between Master and student is this: one knows something and the other is yet to know.

Since this is indeed the case (and from my experience it is), something needs to change. We live in a worldwide community of millions of spiritual seekers, many of which have studied and practiced for years...decades. So, naturally, the thought arises, with almost a half century of direct access to the spiritual teachings of the

East, where are the burgeoning generations of the newly enlightened? Many might say we are still 'spiritually gestating' — our inner child is just waiting to pop out. In deference to the work of the beautiful saints and gurus who have humbly and powerfully graced our shores, I think it is more likely that our inner child may have been in the throws of infancy or adolescence; and the great souls that have come came to nurture us through our formative years in the direction of spiritual puberty. Clearly, with the energetics of our times and the spiritual knowledge that is coming to light, it's time for our inner child to grow up.

So how do we become 'spiritually mature' and what does it mean?

It means knowing who you are and what you are here on this planet to do. 'Knowing who you are' is *not* about knowing your shortcomings, though it's part of the process of coming to know yourSelf. Neither is it a matter of becoming *perfect*. 'Perfect' is, in fact, an ironically relative term; it implies the highest thing *in comparison to everything else*. In truth, *everything* is already perfect...and, at the same time, there isn't any *thing* that *is* Perfection itself, so any substantive attempt at comparison is futile. In the Vedic tradition, 'Perfection' is known by the name *Brahman*. It is in *and* beyond the realm of form...it is everything, and more: it is the Abstract *and* the Abstract-within-form; it is everything *and* no thing...*Nothing*...*-ness,* most often characterized as *Satchitananda* — *Absolute Bliss Consciousness* — by those who've directly experienced it. And yet, even a saint is not an 'Absolute' authority (a real saint will straightforwardly tell you this), even with their vast knowledge and experience. There is always more to know.

As discussed in the chapter on 'Modern Myth Interpretations', each of us, including every saint, has his/her own dharma. Mother Meera, a beautiful saint now living in Germany, was once asked if she knew everything. She looked quizzical. The question was further clarified with another, Did she know, for example, what President Clinton had for breakfast? She just laughed.

Look, it doesn't take omniscience to know stuff. If you want to know something like that, just ask his cook. In the depths of spirituality, you know what you need to know — including the past, present, and future — to do what you're here to do. And, that doesn't mean only supernatural things. You still tie your shoes, pay your bills, wipe your nose, and help your fellow Man. The difference is, instead of being victims of circumstance, you are master of them.

There is no *one* path for all, but there is a spiritual path for everyone. While your path may resemble another's (or many others') path, yours is uniquely yours. No one else can walk it for you. No one else can take your place. Once you've mastered it, you've become the best *you* there can be, without comparison, without equal. You become a Realized expression of the Divine. But, you've always been and will always be unique.

Mystic living is, thus, all-encompassing *and* practical. One time, my brother, who was in the throws of becoming 'born again' at the time, once challenged me/my teachings by saying 'enlightenment' didn't exist because it wasn't spoken of in the Bible. I asked if we could check it out together, read the Bible and see (we'd been relatively estranged prior to that time and it seemed a good chance to talk and be together). Besides, perhaps he was right. To establish common ground, I agreed that the Bible represented God's Word. So, we started with Genesis, page one. Mistranslations aside, we read about these important men who were born, begat so many progeny, did this or that, and died. Again and again, a noted progenitor was born, begat so-and-so, lived so many years and died. Then, came Enoch. His story was much the same, except for the ending. In the end, Enoch *walked with God, and was not.* I said, "There it is!" I commented that in the Vedic teachings 'enlightenment' was described as a conscious connection with the Divine…walking with God…and that saints according to the Vedic tradition did not 'die' (with the focus on the end of the physical form), but 'dropped their body', implying a more conscious act; thus, a saint did not die, but simply left….*was not,* in biblical terms. Truth is truth. In spirituality, it is about how much you really know (directly experience and your *subsequent* understanding of your experience) that matters, not what angle you come to it from.

In our Divine Lineage (the direct line of spiritual Masters), my Master calls Jesus 'the Big Boss'. In an illustrious line, which dates back to the primordial guru, Dattatreya, and includes my Master's Master, Shirdi Sai Baba, as well as Ramana Maharshi, and Ramakrishna Paramahamsa. I thought that was quite a thing. Truth is truth.

So, what is the truth about Jesus' teachings? What of his life, his spiritual journey? Some believe he went to India, studied there (and other places), and got some beautiful things. Others don't. Still others are holding out for more 'proof', which in time will come. One thing is sure: he — all saints, shamans, rishis, avatars, etc. — came on this earth in human form; each gained some depth of command over the forces of nature and learned (often showed) some extraordinary things. They lived, they loved, they walked this earth…and they walked with God. So, how to do this? This book is about everything you ever hoped was true — at least it's about everything I ever hoped was true…about the world…about life…and it actually *being* true. And, it's about how to directly experience it.

The next question rightly is, "How long…how long does it take?" For the last 30 years, I took what I came to describe as the 'natural' machinations of the spiritual process and the nature of the passage of time in this *KaliYuga* to mean 'at a snail's pace'. With few exceptions (already Realized Masters being one), it seemed the process was a life-long (or lifetimes-long) thing. And so, to some degree, like most everyone I knew, I accepted it. It was theoretically/philosophically available any minute, but the practical, common experience was more probably 'later-than-sooner'. After all, the great and ancient sage Vishvamitra meditated for 1,000 years, made a brief misstep and lost his spiritual prowess, and then meditated again before he won his process, then cognized the great *Gayatri* mantra. In any event, it appeared that this was simply the nature of things; that which we long for most must, by nature or Divine Plan, remain faraway — perhaps not inaccessible, but 'out there' nonetheless. However, appearances are deceiving. And, Nature is nothing if not *ironic*. Yes, there is some practical value in judging a book by its cover; yet, in truth there is greater value, immense value, in diving into the world between the cover graphics and the end page and finding out what's what. In this case, in spirituality, it makes all the difference.

Like most people I've known over the last three decades, I spent a fairly good amount of time in meditation (easily thousands of hours), had some rather lovely 'inner' experiences, learned a fair amount of quotable Sanskrit along the way, and gained a bit more insight into the workings of the Universe — at least enough to share my 'wisdom' with others in a way that seemed to inspire and uplift them. Still, for a long time, I didn't realize *the* quantum leap along my spiritual path — the longed-for 'final lifting of the veil of Illusion', neither in myself nor in those I met, nor in those I taught or healed.

Many of my personal experiences were powerful: periodic direct 'inner' experiences of the Divine, the growth of abilities to clearly see bits-and-pieces of the past, present and future, and a substantive increase in the energy to heal others, physically, emotionally, mentally and seemingly even soulfully. But, real, direct knowledge of the inner mechanics of my experiences — and by extension the deeper inner mechanics of nature — were still sketchy, to me: the experiences I did have were real, not hallucinations or wishful-thinking, there was no doubt; my abilities to heal seemed to grow 'naturally' and substantively when channeled through ancient techniques I learned from marvelous, beautiful Masters. But, there too, after some time I inevitably felt I'd hit a ceiling: at one point, for every 4-5 people I would heal in a day, I'd need 7-10 hours to 'come down' from the experience, to de-charge the negative energy I'd 'imbibed' through the healing. I absolutely felt there was more 'out there' (translation: more 'inside me'), but I saw no real way to tap into it. Even though the people who came to me for help responded extraordinarily well (in their words), for me, that unscratchable soulful itch to *really* reach, to know, to hold and to offer more of the healing bliss of the Divine became another in a long line of exercises in patience and surrender to the slow, grinding grip of *MahaKala*, the Lord of Time.

Then, in 2001, on a trip back from India to the US via Frankfurt, my life took an extraordinary turn. During the second leg of that trip (on a flight I wasn't scheduled to be on) I sat next to a beautiful soul (she wasn't scheduled for that flight either; her Master told her she had to take it). Anyway, she handed me a newly published book about the relationship between Eastern wisdom and Western minds, a treatise based on the words of a young Indian saint. Soon after, through the grace of the Divine, I found myself sitting at his feet, and my life truly began a new chapter.

Many of the common spiritual-isms that I had bore witness to were soon washed away. "Every divine soul walks through the same door: mastery of the cosmic forces [in Vedic terms, the *panchabhutas*, 'the Five Elements']. Yes, Shirdi Baba is great. Jesus is great. Ramana Maharshi and Ramakrishna Paramahamsa are great. When will you be this great? That is the important question," he said. "The knowledge I teach comes directly from the ancient palm leaf books," he continued. Although he is a man (a young man) who has performed hundreds of miracles and healed thousands of people, he said humbly, "This is not my creation, this knowledge. It comes from the ancient *maharishis*. Now, it is time for this knowledge to come out." It is the gift of our generation. The time is ripe. Our souls are ripe.

Along with spiritual processes using 'sacred formulas', this beautiful saint lays great emphasis on Vaastu, the ancient science of Vedic architecture. "Vaastu is 50% of spirituality. In your lives, it can solve 80% of your problems. Change your Vaastu and you change your life. That is a spiritual law."

So, once again, we come back to our own backyard. It doesn't matter if you want to go deeply into your spiritual process and win it or whether instead you wish just to live a beautiful life with your friends and family. Here is the deeper, truer point, the crux. If there is an ancient and modern revelation — certainly for us with God on our minds and blossoming in our hearts — it is this: here is an ancient, practical blueprint for structuring fulfillment, for living life masterfully...for changing the world...to bring peace on earth and goodwill towards all humankind...to have real success, peace, harmony, and power in our lives, today, not just in some distant, glorious future.

If there's to be a new Age, it won't be built on myth or mystic confusion or any kind of spiritual slavery, nor will it be simply a milder form of the so-called 'nature' of this Dark Age, based on fear and heartbreak. If there is to be a new Age, it will be built on Vaastu and, in turn, on the firm foundation of our own spiritual mastery...and it will be everything you...everything we...hope the world and our lives can be.

— 2 November, 2005, Penukonda, India.

CHAPTER 1

BUILDING CASTLES IN THE SKY…
AND OTHER PRACTICAL MATTERS

When the Master's peace
is a wild one, my Friend,
the stars all smile…again.
The darkened nights
all tumble in the end
of the Master's peace, my Friend.

from *My Friend*

You visit some friends' house. They've just had a fight. Not while you were there, but before you came in, there was a heated argument. Still, you can feel it; you can cut the tension with a knife. Why? They're done. They're even smiling at you. Still, you can feel it. Is it their body language? Sure, one part, you can see some residue in their eyes, their manner. But, clearly there's more. It's in the air.

What makes the tension hang there? What makes it palpable, even in the face of floor-to-ceiling Pantone® pastels, quietly offset by pale marble end tables topped with crystalline vases, each adorned with a single stalk of freesia in counterpoint to the demure, amber silk lampshades, the subtle-yet-intricate Persian rug, and the wall-to-wall bleached mahogany floors? And why, when we have a fight, do we very often 'retreat' to another room — a favorite room: a bedroom, bathroom, library/den — or 'out for some air'? It is exactly the case that we need a change of atmosphere because the room, the space itself, is holding that aggravated, aggressive, negative energy…and naturally so. The fundamental configurations of a room — the 'directional' (north, south, east, west) floor plan of the walls, entrances, windows, and further, the placement of furniture, etc. — all conscribe as well as hold or support the natural energetic of the space within its walls; and it supports, enhances, or (so sorry) antagonizes the planned or major use/uses the room is put to. According to Vaastu, if the floor plan is 'directionally' unsound, and the use of the room is counter-productive to the natural energetic of that particular space, then it'll take much more than a cool lamp, nice colors, and a smartly-placed mirror to counterbalance it. Conversely, if the room is directionally sound, and is made proper use of, it not only won't support the negativity you might've carried into it with you after a rough day out in the world, it'll sooth, even eliminate it.

Let's start remembering these fundamental terms:

VAASTU:
• 5 Elements
• 16 Directions
• 4 Principles
• Infinite Applications

These are with you wherever you go. Once you grasp them (and you will), you can apply them to every place you've ever been or will be, with amazing results. Let's begin. First, we start with the 'Pillars of Creation', the five Elements.

SPACE: THE ONLY FRONTIER

Space is everywhere. It is the 'field' on and in which all the other elements play. In Sanskrit — the language of the Vedas — space is called *akasha*. But, the word 'space' doesn't really do *akasha* justice. There are too many minimizing connotations, mostly relating to

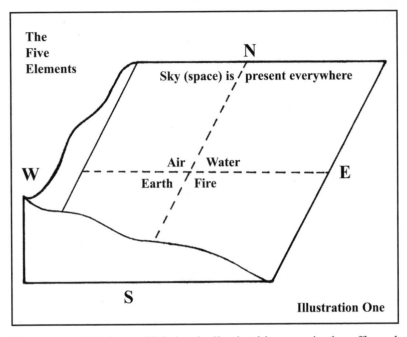

The
Five
Elements

N

Sky (space) is / present everywhere

W

Air / Water
Earth / Fire

E

S

Illustration One

limiting or defining, which ironically, in this case, is the effectual antithesis to the truer meaning of *akasha*. My Master's Vaastu more profoundly uses the word, 'Sky': it is vast; it touches everything and is found everywhere; it carries amazing things in it — some visible to us, some invisible; all vibrations (implying everything that possesses a form, no matter how gross or subtle) exist within it and leave a trace when they take form in it. All the science — it is the home of pure potentiality and, when acted upon, can manifest — and esoterica — *omniscience* is a matter of opening a conscious channel to the akashic records in which knowledge of everything that travels through it is available — indicate that it is fundamental to all existence. It is the underlying field in which the seeds *of everything* — energy in all its forms — were, are, and will be planted and made manifest. It is the fundamental building block.

Simply by existing in this world, to some degree you access and directly experience the sway of this enormous cosmic power, which influences the physical, emotional, material and spiritual worlds around and within you. But, how is it harnessed...so that we can access deeper levels of success, happiness, physical, mental and emotional health and wellbeing, and spiritual enlightenment? To harness the sky element, we have to channel it — set parameters through which the energy can be held and within which it can flow. To do this in terms of homes, offices, buildings, and properties, we build walls.

How the walls are set/established (along the lines of the compass, etc.) conscribes and 'identifies' the energetic character of a building, room, or property. That's why, for example, when building according to Vaastu on a new property, we always start by building compound or property walls with the proper alignment to harness the infinite harmonizing potential of the Sky Element within the new property. In this way, the stage is set for optimizing the tremendous power of Nature through the 'placement' and use of the other four Elements: Earth, Fire, Water, and Air.

Mother's earth, I've sat upon
and talked to the sky
from dusk 'til dawn.
And all-the-while,
He's carried on
to bring us Home...again.

EARTH: THE LOVER, THE MOTHER, THE MAGNET & THE WALL

Each of the Five Elements has its own profound qualities, character, and expressions, and is invaluable in the fundamental energetic makeup of the world/cosmos. The Vedic sciences deal with both the vastness and the intimacy of Nature — all to shed light on the source, course, and goal, and the profound intricacies of our relationship with it. According to the Vedic wisdom, we have an extraordinarily intimate connection with *everything* in the cosmos because everything is based upon the same foundation: the universal foundation of the Five Elements. Everything is made of the same energetic stuff. Everything that comes in a body, a form, is under the sway of the Five Elements. Even when God came to earth — in the forms of Lord Krishna, Lord Rama, and others — he took a body; and that body lived and loved and walked, worked and laughed within the dominion of the Five Elements.

As the intimacy of this relationship grows, they gain a commanding on the energy. It may be said, this command of nature is one of the main characteristics of the saints. And, what they have done, each of us can do. Externally, through Vaastu, it is easy to structure this harmonious intimacy with Nature in the worls/environment around us.

So, in terms of our external and internal 'environments', how do we gain a commanding on these Pillars of Creation? When it comes to their personal spiritual paths, the saints charge the energy of the Elements directly to their souls, which means structuring channels to create a lasting, naturally power-charged familiarity with each Element — thus establishing a more intimate 'best friends' relationship with Nature. In time, they come to recognize how to channel the energy so that it expresses itself more harmoniously in, around, and through. Vaastu makes it possible for each of us to live in a truly 'sacred' space — an environment that is *most supportive* for our *highest* success, our *greatest* happiness, and the fulfillment of our desires in the world. Charging the Five Elements to your soul expands the parameters to include the greater depths of spirituality.

To understand the characteristics of the Earth Element, let's take as example the earth itself. The earth nourishes all life. It provides abundant food and shelter. We plant seeds and from the earth comes fruits, flowers, plants, vegetables...all the gifts *and more* that a lover brings — all of which are Her gifts to us. She is home-and-hearth to our species and a billion others. The earth is fecund, emblematic of creative energy, creative power. From ancient times to today, we've recognized this terrestrial orb as an amazing gift-giver, and have named her as a physical embodiment of the divine *Shakti*, a form of Mother Divine herself. In the Vedic tradition, G.O.D. stands for Generator/Creator, Operator/Maintainer, and Destroyer. Certainly, all these names can also apply to Mother Earth.

Even when we abuse her, she still gives us Her bounty. But, Mother doesn't *always* appear convivial or respond...kindly. The earth has huge destructive as well as creative power. Just in recent years, we've had dozens of devastating earthquakes around the world, as well as other natural disasters. This natural, worldwide turmoil and upheaval is partly manmade. In many ways and for many years we have pushed the limits of Mother's 'good hostess' nature, attempting to manipulate crop growth, massive animal/food populations, weather conditions (rainfall, etc.) and more — directly poking and prodding Her, testing Her resistance. But, even more incessant has been our energetic onslaught on Nature, via the levels of human fear, hate, confusion, blame, jealousy, and greed which are very much apparent and unabated, infesting every nation, every community, and every home. How long do you think Mother will stand for that? Recently, we've seen direct indications. The world is a closed system (despite holes in the ozone). Agitation and aggravation breed pressure. There are energetic limits before the pressure erupts. And, therefore, it's worth our while to handle Her (and each other) lovingly, harmoniously, to also bring Her peace.

The real commanding on any and all of the Elements comes not from abuse or *control* — make a big note: 'commanding on' is not 'control' — but comes from being able to handle the energy in a beautiful way. Energetically you become, let us say, such super close friends that Nature wants to please you, as a good friend, to support you. And so, naturally, the energy responds to what you do/want in a more harmonious way. What we do with Vaastu is create a situation wherein Nature is inspired to support us in every aspect of our lives.

Besides being quite giving, Mother Earth is hugely receptive. If we look into the mechanics of this quality of receptivity, we see that the Earth Element is highly magnetic. It possesses the amazing energy to attract, absorb and hold — it can draw and hold the Divine energy and it can suck or wash the negativity.

In ancient traditions, including the Vedic tradition, you can readily see the use of the Five Elements in temples and holy rituals and ceremonies: the Fire is present in the lamp flame and the smoke of the lit incense; the Air is there, made 'visible' as the smoke wafts and the light flickers before the icon or holy symbol; and the icon itself — in the Vedic tradition, the icon is called a *murti* — is made of earth; Water is evident by the regular, daily *abhishek* (bath) given to the *murti* and by the water/liquid given into the hands of the attendees at the end of the gathering as part of the *prasad* (divine fruits of the offering, presentation, or ritual/ceremony). All are there.

The murti — the holy icon, itself — is made of Earth. When you go to a temple in India, for example, like the one in Sri Sailam, each day you will find thousands of devotees coming to visit the murti inside. In Sri Sailam, the murti/icon within the huge temple is a small, black, 'stone' *Shivalingam* (said to be of super-natural origin), itself less than a foot in height. Adishankara (a great saint, the reviver of the Vedic tradition subsequent to the coming of the Buddha, and founder of the Swami order in India) is known to have visited this 'small' object centuries ago — as have hundreds, perhaps thousands of saints since its installation there. What is the inner mechanism? What is the attraction?

Firstly, is it possible it is of divine (super-natural) origin? Yes. But, let's say it is natural. Being made of the Earth Element, it has the power to draw and hold divine energy — perhaps transmitted by a saint (or saints) — and which, by its own Earth Element nature, can give/transmit blessings and draw, wash or release the negative energy from those who touch it. Hundreds of millions of people have visited this small stone over past generations. More than a million visit it each year, to this day. You would think with such huge numbers, if there was no direct experience, even cultural bias could not sustain them coming back generation after generation; the numbers would diminish. But, that is not the case.

The life-size, living 'statue' of *Lord Venkateshwara* in the South-Indian town of Tirupati is another example. It is housed in a village-size compound and enclosed in a temple literally covered in gold. *Darshan* of Him (seeing the murti with your own eyes) is an extraordinary experience. But, to do so, people stand in line for hours...*often, for days*...with thousands of others — on high holy days, over a hundred thousand is a regular occurrence — for the chance to see Him for 15-20 seconds before the priests move each person past and out of the viewing area. The visitors are so moved by the experience that they not only spend their time and the effort it takes to see Him, but the offerings they give are such that the Golden Temple is the richest temple in India. It is said that on high holy days, the gifts of gold, money, and precious items are so abundant that the attendants use shovels to gather them from around the overflowing *hundhi* (offering bins). The murti is, of course, the real attraction. But, the founder of the temple, the saint-king Krishnadevaraya, wanted to make additional assurances for the temple's success and longevity, so he had it all built according to Vaastu. This he did over four hundred years ago. So far, so good.

The Earth Element is known to be the hardest to command upon because it in itself has huge commanding energy. It can hold enormous amounts of energy, even in a small compact form, such as the lingam in Sri Sailam. This Element can be used to confer amazing positive energy or it can protect you from negativity by drawing it from you and into itself. But, the Earth Element can also protect in another way. It can keep negative energy out. These are part of the inner mechanics, according to Vaastu, of constructing compound or property walls. One part, walls made of the Earth Element conscribe the property inside; but they also separate and protect the property from the variant energies outside. So, in general, according to Vaastu the Earth Element has a three-fold value: it sets the parameters for the energy of a property; it holds that energy, structuring the ongoing energetic integrity of the property; and, it protects the property and the inhabitants from outside negativity, while helping to release or 'de-charge' the negative energy within them. This is (one of the many reasons) why, when a property, home, apartment, or office has good Vaastu, it is naturally and literally 'whole' or holy, a sacred space.

FIRE: LIGHT, HEAT & TRANSFORMATION

One of my earliest childhood memories is of seeing a cartoon cricket happily warming himself on the cartoon hearth in front of a blazing cartoon fire while chatting with his wooden friend, an Italian cartoon kid named Pinocchio. I used to do the same thing, except I would sit (though there was no wooden kid — cartoon, Italian or otherwise) with my back to the blaze until it got so hot I thought my shirt would catch fire, then I'd turn and sit on the floor, lean on the granite hearth, and watch the flames lick the logs, which would crackle in return. My favorite part, though, was gazing into the embers beneath the burning logs, my face warm and red, like them. Fire 'means' all that: warmth, friendship, light, brightness, color, joy, song and dance, peace, security…and home. And, more: it means cooking and romance and solitude and sharing, family, and introspection, enlightenment, wisdom, transformation…and life. It is the embodiment of dynamism, substantive yet etheric, soothing yet dangerous, and very, very powerful. The Light-of-lights in this corner of the cosmos is the Sun, without which no living thing here would exist. It may not be the only building block required for life, but it is the cornerstone.

In Vedic astrology — called *Jyotish*, which itself means 'light' — the Sun is characterized as the Soul-of-souls, the Progenitor, the Lord of everything that exists between the earth and sky. The Vedic *Puranas* (literally, 'old stories' or histories) deem him the celestial embodiment of *MahaVishnu*, the divine Universal Support, from whose navel *Brahma*, the Creator, was born. Vedic astrology is a fascinating and intricate science, with many extraordinary aspects, one of which is the prescription of energetic remedies to mitigate past karma. Of these, some of the most powerful are *yagyam*, fire ceremonies. Specific materials are offered into the fire, while *mantras* (sacred formulas) are chanted. The Fire transforms and transmits the energy/vibrations of the offerings into the environment, changing your personal 'vibratory' makeup and your energetic relationship with the subtle forces in the environment that bring your karma back to you. Connection with the Fire Element changes/enhances your soul capacity and turns the negative energy in and around you to 'ash', so to speak

Proper 'placement' of the Fire Element can sooth and nurture the inhabitants, optimize the mind-body connection, and increase physical health as well as mental/emotional wellbeing. Poorly placed, it can 'cook' the family…especially women. There is a particular universal dynamic between the Fire Element and the Divine Feminine, which the extraordinary gift of being a woman embodies. The nature of the Fire is *transformational*. Within the female energy/form, *the spark of life* resides, which the seed of existence (a male's sperm) is impotent without. She possesses the creative power. With it, she can transform a miniscule, squiggly, polliwog-of-a-thing into a physiological monument-of-a-temple that can house a doctor, lawyer, Indian *Raj*...or a saint.

This immense connection with the Fire Element is one reason why women actively took up the task of cooking, of working so closely with it — because, like so many things, they could naturally do it better. But, when we don't honor the natural energetics involved in the process of working with nature, such as following the directional strengths of the Element, the positive connection (the channel) and resulting benefits are diminished, even to the point of causing discomfort, pain, and sorrow.

Fire does burn. Forests are laid waste. Anger fuels hatred and distorts passion. Excessive heat readily turns violent and destructive. All are a far cry from visions of a cricket on the hearth. But, to some degree, they are the common, even daily experience. The degree to which they are characteristic of our lives can be traced back to the quality of our Vaastu. The nearer we come as individuals and as a race to reinstituting the harmonies of nature in the lives we lead — done easily by reinvigorating the places where we sleep and breathe — the closer we come to true holistic living. And, the sooner the better.

WATER: THE BOAT, THE NET & THE BOOMBOX

80% of our planet is covered in water. 80% of the body is made up of water. It follows then that 80% of the Illusion is carried in the Water Element. In Sanskrit, the web or net of the Cosmic Illusion in which we live is often called *Mayajal...Maya* (Illusion), *jal* (water). Charging and commanding on the Water Element is a large part of gaining mastery over the Illusion. Lord Krishna is a great historic example, for he was a quintessential master of the Illusion. An *avatar* ('descended one') of *MahaVishnu*, he was the illustrious, hereditary scion of the Lunar Dynasty. The moon rules the tides, their ebb and flow. Its light is cooling, in contrast with the intense heat of the sun. And, its light is reflective, which is emblematic of the Illusion itself: it is not the Reality, but a mirror image of It, a reflection. Water is a carrier. In its currents the illusions flow, like a boat on a river. We can say the Water Element is a carrier, a conductor, of a large portion of the energy that flows through our lives. And, therefore, its influence is also dramatic in the warp-and-woof of our daily existence as well as on the broader journey we make along the path of our soul.

Lord Krishna was known to have an amazing ability to hook the female energy. He had amazing channels to connecting to that. Through the sounds emanating from his flute, he would capture the hearts of the female cow-herders as they sat nearby or bathed in the river. Later, as a conquering prince and king, he had 16,000 consorts, each of whom would boast night-after-night that He had spent the entire night alone with them in conjugal love, in bliss. There is a similar story of *MahaVishnu*, Himself: when the *amruta* (nectar of immortality) was created, in order to ensure the *devas* (celestial gods) got it and the *asuras* (demons) did not, He took the form of *Mohini,* the most beautiful of women, and distracted the demons, allowing the *devas* to drink the nectar, become immortal, and defeat the *asuras* in battle. Also, MahaVishnu-as-Mohini attracted the amorous attentions of Lord Shiva, which culminated in the creation of *Ayyappa*, a human child with celestial attributes who aided in the destruction of the commanding forces of negativity.

Okay, perhaps that was a bit too much ancient history all at once. But, it wasn't meant as a diversion. Interwoven in those stories are the inner characteristics and the fragrance of the Water Element. When you charge the Water Element, the negative agitations of Nature (of the Illusion) are cooled and calmed. While the Water Element carries 80% of the illusions, it also has a huge capacity to channel/conduct/carry the Divine energy as well. But, more than that, it has the capacity to amplify the energy it conducts.

Water carries/conducts...*and amplifies...energy.*

If the Water Element is placed or flows improperly, it will carry that misaligned distortion and amplify it. But, when properly placed, it generates tranquility, transmits huge healing energy, and amplifies the wisdom, grace, joy, love, and abundance in your life. It's a kind of divine nectar.

AIR: MIND OVER MATTER

You can go without food for weeks, even months. You can go for days without water. But, air...in only a few minutes, you're *swaha,* finished, adios-ed. Like water, air is a conductor — only, it's really, really fast! And, air is super potent: it carries extraordinary energy in it. In Sanskrit, one of the words for 'air' is *prana,* which also means 'life force'.

The Air Element is very much associated with movement, communication and, therefore, also with the mind. We all know how quickly our minds can change, how we can become easily distracted, confused, afraid, shocked, or elated. The characteristics of the Air Element, then, also carry an emotional impact.

The Air Element also has a particularly intimate association with the Sky (space/*akasha*) Element. To a large extent, from our two-feet-on-the-ground, first-person perspective, they are one and the same — but, not exactly. All the knowledge in the universe may reside in the Sky, but our ability to assimilate it, through our intelligence — through the innate characteristic of intelligence — and to express it, comes via the Air Element. The natural 'home' (proper placement) of the Air Element fosters intelligence, mental acuity, and discrimination. It structures tranquility, but disallows lethargy. Since it has a great influence on the quality and depth of our mental (and emotional) state, it has a strong impact on our dreams as well. And, it allows for the awakening and growth of creative intelligence, which is a special category/flavor of consciousness.

Once it is charged to our soul, through spiritual processes, the Air Element's powerful healing energy can be transmitted over long distances very quickly. When properly placed according to Vaastu, the Air Element ensures financial stability and growth, even increase in social status and fame, as well as neutralizes the occurrence of legal difficulties. This doesn't mean you'll automatically become a Madonna, Bill Gates or Elton John — you are and will always be...you. But, improving your Vaastu means you enhance the experience of knowing who you are and living your unique life in a beautiful way. One of the special perks of alignment with the Air Element is that the process moves more quickly and easily.

What happens if we mis-place the Air Element? Instead of feeling 'at home', it would be agitated; and, as a natural by-product, would express itself in that way, through us and to us, via the world around us. Gauge your own life — your own (forgive me) monkey-mind — and the level of 'balanced' or 'well-rounded' intelligence you see displayed in the world. Would you say in general and in particular that there is a perceivable (much less, harmonious) alignment with this Pillar of Creation, the Air Element? In the Vedas it says that 'enlightenment' — a broad term for the highest stages of human existence — can be known and lived with each breath. Do you know how many times we inhale and exhale every day? Roughly 28,000 times. So, if you were to gauge, in these terms, what would be the number for you...how many times a day do you inhale and exhale your full potential, and experience, utilize, and express your innate divine intelligence?

Einstein put it another way. It is said that when he spoke of us living our full potential he felt that even so-called 'geniuses' (himself included) were using only/possibly 5-10% of their full potential. So, what of the rest of us? 1%? 2-3%? That implies that in his very discriminating opinion, the best of us were living 90-95% *in ignorance.* How much would the numbers jump, do you think, if we lived aligned with the very energetic of the transmission and expression of intelligence — and Cosmic Intelligence at that? How would life be lived if the percentages of manifest intelligence and ignorance were reversed? The words 'heaven on earth' easily come to mind.

In the meantime, it does seem that much of our life is colored (if not dominated) by our 'monkey mind'. Do you know where that expression comes from? Of course, it's easy from one angle to connect the dots: we have the recognizable primate-simian connection; plus, there is the monkey's natural tendency to jump from branch to branch again and again; couple that with a very evident short attention span, and the analogy easily hits home. But, let me also add an ancient, more positive, and spiritual spin on this.

Hanuman, the 'monkey-god' — he's actually a *vanar,* of an ancient, highly intelligent, missing-link kind of race between man and monkey — was also called *Vayuputra,* 'son of the Wind'. You can read about his life and exploits in any number of renditions of the story of his beloved Lord Rama, *the Ramayana.* But, I want to quickly mention three deeper points here. The first: *Hanuman* was so lively, inquisitive, and inspired that it came to the ever-moving *Surya* (the sun) to be his guru. The second: Lord Rama wanted 'to know' how his wife Sita was — she had been kidnapped by Ravana, the king of the Asuras, and taken across the sea to Lanka, his island-fortress. So, Hanuman offered to go and report back. Lord Rama agreed and, without a second thought, only the thought, *"Ram...Ram...Ram..."* on his mind (and in his heart), Hanuman leapt into the air and across the sea to Lanka, where he assured Sita that her husband loved her before he returned home (but only after setting much of Lanka ablaze). The third point: as the final battle raged between the armies of Lord Rama and those of Ravana, the slaughter could be seen everywhere. Something had to be done. An herbal decoction, which was known to have huge healing abilities (it could even raise the dead), had to be brought to the battlefield to revive Lord Rama's forces. Once again, Hanuman leapt to the task; soaring through the air across the length and breadth of the Indian subcontinent, he procured the herbs and brought them back to Lord Rama (not wanting to waste precious time, Hanuman actually scooped up the whole mountain and brought it back with him). Each of these stories highlights the Air Element and illustrates many of its sublime qualities and characteristics: knowledge, intelligence, communication, power, speed, the ease of crossing great distances and overcoming even greater obstacles; and, further, they also express deeper characteristics such as compassion, one-pointed devotion, and selfless service. A Pillar of Creation, indeed.

EARTH: commanding, absorbing, protective, magnetic
FIRE: nurturing, warming, brilliant, transformative
SKY: omnipresent, omniscient, creative
WATER: purifying, a carrier/transmitter, amplifying
AIR: a super-fast carrier/transmitter, associated with intelligence, the mind & *prana,* the life force

The *Panchabhutas*, the Five Elements, taken individually are still like facets on a diamond — together they make up a gem that is brilliant from every angle. Like that, they work individually and collectively. If on one's property one is poorly placed or mismanaged, the others are compromised as well. The same holds true when we speak of their balance and expressions within us. So, while we deal with them individually when discussing them, but practical application dictates that they also be addressed and accommodated as a collective whole. Otherwise, your life and your karma will be adversely affected, now and for some time into the future.

It is the same when we refer to charging the Five Elements to our souls, through spiritual practices. While we may charge them one at a time, they're not completely charged until all five are charged. This is another primary facet to the meaning of 'holistic'; in spiritual terms, this is the real substance of 'all-encompassing'.

CHAPTER 2

RELATIVE ABSOLUTES & MODERN MYTH INTERPRETATIONS

In the darkness of the night,
when the moon begins to rise,
Shiva sighs.
When the starlit winds run wild
and the fires kiss the sky,
Shiva sighs.
Om Nama Shivaya!
Om Jai Jai Mahadev!

THE THING ABOUT SPIRITUAL LAWS

"There are no absolutes in the Relative [our world/realm of name-and-form], except the Absolute [Brahman/the Divine Unbounded/God, the Impersonal] itself," the saying goes. Every law in nature — including every super-natural/spiritual one — is, in all its manifest permutations, a 'relative absolute': which means, with the passage of time, even though they remain fundamentally, even recognizably the same, their expressions and even some (or many) of their components change, *including how to access them*. It's important to recognize that it's not just our understanding that changes, as in the way Newtonian physics was replaced by Quantum physics, even though the universe continued on its merry way before and after that intellectual/theoretical, scientific breakthrough. Just as cells mutate, plants and animals adapt, and societies shift and grow, yet retain a semblance of themselves, spiritual laws also change over time: the ways to access them, the requirements for applying them, and what it takes to manifest their results in our lives, and how to build upon them — these change. For anyone intent on enhancing their life, and certainly for those on a spiritual path, it's important to really digest this point: the valuable (yet, perhaps still adolescent) contributions of modern science notwithstanding, it is the spiritual laws that most influence our conscious connection with the sublime energetics of nature, which constantly influence us; in practical not just esoteric terms, they are the ones that most profoundly impact our direct, personal experience, and thus can offer the greatest benefit to us, to our family and friends, and to the world.

Often, 'modern' thinkers question the validity of so-called 'ancient thought'. But, Allopathic medicine has been around how long? It could be argued it's been in evidence since Leonardo Da Vinci dissected his first cadaver and made intricate drawings of the human anatomy. Or, we could argue that it was invented and codified by Hippocrates. All fine and good. *Modern* Allopathy, however — in the form we see it has evolved into currently — has been plied for about a hundred years. One of its mainstay safeguards is a set of two to three dozen tests (although, unfortunately, it costs a ton of money to produce them) resulting in 'proven' successes (and, unfortunately, perhaps as many or more…um, unfortunate…side-effects). But, here's the thing with 'ancient' systems, like Ayurveda, the Vedic system of natural (nature-based) healthcare: they've been tried and tested for *thousands* of years, with literally *billions* of cases over generations. You'd think, if it didn't work, you'd know it within 5-6,000 years…which is about the time — yes, that long ago — when this ancient wisdom was first written down. And, by the way, at *that* time it was also called 'ancient wisdom'.

At least one of the seeds of the problem lies in the realm of language/communication: there is a decided lack of modern terminology for the spiritual premises of ancient practices, which the arts and sciences were founded upon. This is coupled and supported by our cultural biases: if a Western client/patient read the ingredient 'uric acid' he or she may or may not think or care much about it (our inbred reliance on authority/experts); but, if the list of ingredients included 'cow's urine' (as many Ayurvedic remedies in India do), they wouldn't hesitate to, well, throw a fit. In Ayurveda, there are also important uses for heavy metals, like mercury, in specified quantities, which produce extraordinary results. But, in the West, so many people have little tolerance (intellectually and quite often now physically), whether through abuse or ignorance, to stray from the black-and-white margins of the modern versions of science, including medicine. And so, sadly, they call for adjustments in the formulas or for throwing them over altogether. Yet, for those who are open to the potential benefits (both spiritual and material) these ancient systems provide, the timely changes that do occur naturally offer amazing opportunities for expansion and positive growth.

When She dances through the night,
there before your eyes,
Shiva sighs…

Every 5,000 years, 2,000 years, 1,000 years, every 500, and every 100 years, spiritual laws change. It's all part of Mother Nature's dance. Nature was so *sattvic* ('pure'/energetically pristine) during the ancient times of the *Saptarishis* (the seven 'original' Great Seers of the Vedic civilization), for example, that the pace of spiritual progress was…slow. The great sage *Vishwamitra* meditated 1,000 years to win his process; but because he broke his diksha (the guidelines for his process), he had to do it again before he actually won it. Today, the laws of nature are such that in this Age we can win our spiritual processes very quickly, in a matter of a few years and, in some cases, in a matter of months. But, the relative absolutes of spirituality must be acknowledged and respected. In effect, they are the same *and* different from past Ages to this.

Still, while precise aspects of the applications may vary, the fundamental truths remain intact. One truth is that there are known rules, which exist and need to be acknowledged and utilized to create the desired results. Following the guidelines is a key ingredient for success. Because the energetics of the laws change, the tools themselves — *mantras*, *yantras*, and *Vaastu*, for example in the Vedic spiritual tradition — are naturally modified to keep pace with these changes in order to produce the highest benefit. Yet, for sticklers of form over substance, let me say, a modern carpenter's nail gun is still, in effect, just a (modified) hammer — the same, yet different. And, it's a valuable, not undermining difference. Like that, knowing and following the rules are important. But, recognizing and applying their naturally-new version can make all the difference. It's worthwhile to take a look at some relative absolutes to see how they've changed and to what result.

I remember the sun burned a hole in the raging sky,
and the ashes flying, filling the night,
the waters that carried the wandering shadows home,
and the stars that
made love to my eyes...

DIKSHA: PROTECTING YOUR PROCESS

This is the Vedic term for 'guideline' — in effect, 'borders of support'; which is to say, the boundaries within which energy is channeled and which aid in the creation of specific energetic results. Each spiritual process has its *diksha* (set of guidelines). When we walk a path in this way, the path itself offers added support to the energy the individual process has to offer (for all you 'path-less-taken' swashbuckler/oddity/exceptions, see the section entitled, IN THE NAME OF DASH & DARE). When we hold to our diksha, success is a lock — winning our process is, one part, automatic. The challenge is in the testings — by Mother Divine Herself, through nature (including our own illusions, our own blocks), and from the lineage of spiritual Masters, including the guru. If seekers (and saints) have 'fallen' it is because they could not hold to their *diksha* in the face of these testings. Ironically, the testings 'hit' through our personal blocks — our fears, jealousies, those limiting aspects/attachments which we hold on to dearly and which hold us back from living our full potential. That's why 'washing our blocks' (our personal shortcomings) is an integral part of the spiritual path. Notice I didn't say *analyzing* our blocks. You don't have to know the circumstantial source or course of them to wash them. After all, the karmic seed that sprouted into heartbreak in this life could have been (and most probably was) planted in a previous one. If we had to know our past lives to achieve the first drop of success in this one, it would probably take us all our waking hours this time around (and next) to do so.

Is there any way to hedge our bets to insure greater progress and success, step-by-step? Yes, Vaastu. Vaastu is 50% of spirituality. Let's say that again:

Vaastu is 50% of spirituality.

When you live, work, and breathe in a good Vaastu environment, the nature itself hugely supports your success, in all endeavors, by enhancing the channels that create success. One natural by-product of living in good Vaastu is the ease and quickened pace of the process of releasing our blocks. This is one of the incredible, fundamental values in following the *dikshas*, the guidelines, of Vaastu. Follow them and

your path becomes quicker and easier. Your progress becomes smooth
and evident, day-by-day.

> I remember from Time to Time...
> I remember the water to wine.
> And, the heart that opened mine.
> And the wild winds that
> dried the tears from my eyes.

> Om Nama Shivaya!
> Om Jai Jai Mahadev!

THE NUANCE OF RULES

Often it is said that poetry is the Mystic's way — Life as poetry.
But, why? One part, the subtleties of Existence are, by nature,
hidden. Since they are also part-and-parcel of the Mystic's life, to
communicate these subtleties and one's personal experiences, the
expressions of those experiences ought to themselves be sublime —
more a 'hinting at' than finger-pointing or check list cataloguing. But,
this angle on spiritual poetics counts only about 2%.

There's an old saying, "What we learn in private, we keep private."
Why? Because...the Illusion will hit. When the positive increases, it
is natural that the negativity will follow. This is our experience, isn't
it? The positive doesn't just last and last, and grow and grow.
Negativity comes to disturb it, waylay it, or to beat it down. It is a
very natural part of spiritual processes that illusions will hit, 'trying'
to disturb your process. If you write (or speak) about your process
'directly' then, the nature will hit directly. Indirect expressions
(hintings/poetry, etc.) divert the negativity away from the process and
back into the nature.

"Last night, while I sat out in the garden charging the Sky Element, an angel came, stood in front of me, and said he'd come to tell me the secrets of the Seven Most Sacred Power Spots of this world. So, naturally, I went and got my pen." If someone read this (or heard this, either first or second hand), his common, initial reaction would be dismissive, and probably wrapped in jealousy. Because we commonly hold on to our own blocks of jealousy, unworthiness, anger, fear, et al, we (yes, especially we in the West) find it difficult to be glad for another's success and/or happiness. When presented with another's depth of experience, the tendency is to throw crap at it.

Absolutely, it's worthwhile to protect your process from this. One part, we build personal protection circles using spiritual practices specific for this purpose; and, certainly, we build personal protection circles whenever we can live/love/work and do our *sadhana* (our spiritual practices) in good Vaastu. But, for anyone at any stage, negativity hits us through our blocks. The thing is, Vaastu dramatically helps mitigate this.

My Master always says it's a hugely beautiful spiritual tool to keep a journal — the poetics of your journey. Remember, whenever you write or speak about your personal experiences, *express/communicate* them in hints. One part, your thoughts, words, and actions carry your *shakti* (spiritual power) in them. That is how they affect the world — by carrying your divine fragrance. They open a direct channel to you, and from you, to the world.

And, isn't it the case that a true Mystic's words are deeply touching? They inspire us. Although we're often set slightly off-balance by them, and rightly so, we are nonetheless moved. Expressing/communicating the sublime in thought, word, and action — as a living example — is part of the mastery of Mystic Living.

Of course, it may sound a bit tricky (as in difficult), begging the question, "So why write about it in the first place?" Firstly, in this way the negativity is diverted away from your process. Secondly, as you go along your spiritual process you pass through the three stages of Illusion. Writing down your experiences help remind you of where you've been and what you've gone through. And, thirdly, if it's done well, there is the possibility that the energy 'thrown' at your words/expressions will itself be positive — even loving, expansive expressions of heartful gratitude. People will respond in a more beautiful way; in effect, enhancing/charging the energy of the words (which are connected to the process), which will increase the success and longevity of the process that gave rise to the words in the first place. It is said Hafiz's Master had him write a poem each day for almost forty years. It was an integral part of his process. What he wrote about *was* his process: he poetically chronicled his experiences, but in such a way that millions of souls have been moved by his words to more deeply open their own hearts, and to be more conscious and loving in their thoughts and deeds. As expressed by the Sufi Master, the whole point of Hafiz's process was to create an unbounded heart. His expressions carry that energetic — they transmit it — so that that same spiritual fire is rekindled in a new heart. As the saying goes, "The light is the same. The candles are many." These are the inner mechanics of *diksha*.

> Om Nama Shivaya!
> Om Jai Jai Mahadev!
> When the morning light has come,
> and His heart your soul has won,
> Shiva sighs.
> — from *Shiva Sighs*

Dikshas — guidelines, boundaries — are invaluable. Keeping within them, you've got immeasurable support. In Vaastu, creating boundaries strengthens the channel(s) for the cosmic energies to run and express themselves in harmonious ways. When set according to Vaastu, the practical result is Heaven-on-Earth.

To the degree we slip or slide around the *dikshas* of Vaastu, to that degree the drama of negativity will run in our lives. It's that simple...and predictable. You can predict a person's karma and coming life-events by checking out the Vaastu of his living and work spaces. Of course, most of us are not in a position to tear everything down and start from scratch. We live in apartments, or houses, in municipalities — urban or suburban — which have long since been in place and continue to grow without any authoritative input from us; and, it's also a safe bet community planners are not yet setting their sights on developing good Vaastu ordinances. But, Vaastu does exist — whether you live in Benares or Pocatello, Idaho — whether a construction crew or local magistrate knows it or not. It's presently hit-or-miss when it comes to living in good Vaastu in the West. But, that's our karma.

And, that's exactly the point. Our karma structures our Vaastu. We are 'drawn' to certain Vaastu — we resonate with it — because of our karma. And, our Vaastu upholds and holds/structures/perpetuates our karma in return. So, here's the point:

Change your Vaastu and you change your karma.

In the preface I mentioned one of the naturally-new changes in one of the relative absolutes of Vaastu: the importance of emphasizing the northeast, and the energetic convergence of the strengths of north and east — north for abundance and financial wealth, and the east for Divine wisdom. In this Age, when we say spirituality is 'practical' we don't mean just for ascetics or priests. It applies to every soul that has taken a human form. In this Age, more than ever, wealth is a viable spiritual tool. It must be wrested from the petty, malicious forces of

Negativity and used for the spiritual upliftment of all. But, this is not going to happen by banging down the doors of some corporate despot and fleecing his accounts. That is an old, tired, and unproductive way. It makes more sense to gather the positive forces of nature into our camp and let nature take its course. In this way, the tide will turn of its own accord — quickly and surely.

In an ideal situation — on open land, for example — the first thing we do to create excellent Vaastu is to build compound walls. We set boundaries. These boundaries hold the dynamic energies of nature to a channel, a channel which activates them in specific ways, and which sets the stage for a (greater) life of poetry. Where we cannot set all the parameters from start-to-finish, we can still discriminate with the help of our understanding of Vaastu to consciously seek out better, more supportive Vaastu. Wherever the Pillars of Creation — Earth, Fire, Sky, Water, and Air — exist, there you can apply Vaastu.

Whatever reality is in existence, by which all the rest subsists, that is Brahman. An Eternal behind all instabilities, a Truth of things, which is implied, if it is hidden in all appearances, a Constant which supports all mutations, but it is not increased, diminished, abrogated — there is such an unknown X which makes existence a problem, our own self a mystery, the universe a riddle. If we were only what we seem to be to our normal self-awareness, there would be no mystery; if the world were only what it can be made out to be by the perceptions of the senses and their strict analysis in the reason, there would be no riddle; and if to take our life as it is now and the world as it has so far developed to our experience were the whole possibility of our knowing and doing, there would be no problem. At best, there would be but a shallow mystery, an easily solved riddle, the problem only of a child's puzzle. But, there is more, and that more is the hidden head of the Infinite and the secret heart of the Eternal. It is the highest and this highest is the all; there is none beyond and there is none other than it.

— Sri Aurobindo

(commentary on the Taittriya Upanishad from *The Upanishads, Part One* by Sri Aurobindo, published 1971, 1981, 2000 by Sri Aurobindo Ashram, Pondicherry, INDIA)

MODERN MYTH INTERPRETATIONS

The words above were written by a wonderful, holy man from India, who displayed a unique dexterity with language and possessed an inherent plasticity of experience. Together, he used these to clarify the ancient spiritual wisdom propagated by the Vedic literature and in Vedic terms, and to support and advance the progress of the spiritual process itself, in whichever way one came to it, for whoever heard the call. The specific aspect he is commenting on here is the foundation-of-all-foundations, *Brahman*, the Absolute. Yet, even this is a controversial subject. Many propound that Brahman is 'all and everything', and that the world as we know it is an 'illusion', meaning it does not really exist. Others counter by saying if Brahman is 'all', then there can be nothing other than Brahman, meaning nothing can exist outside of It; therefore, since the world/universe is of/a part of Brahman, it exists — it is real. The number of varying opinions on the nuances of this is probably about equal to the number of people who consider the subject in the first place. Why? Because everyone bases their opinions on the subject on their personal understanding and experience, or their lack of it.

In Vedic understanding, there are two ways to gain knowledge, *shruti* and *shmriti:* you take someone's word for it (you hear of it or read it in a book); or it comes from direct experience — in spiritual terms, this means through or including divine revelation. Often, the instructions given (like in the case of the *dikshas*) come from those with immense, direct spiritual experience who have tested their 'inner research' in themselves and in the world and recorded the results and applications for posterity. But, now, in our Age this situation has become a double-edged sword. Once, these accounts were considered mythic — awe-inspiring, humbling, worthy of respect, a spur to better action. Now, they are considered mere myth — false...or too removed from practical experience. So, today, we are cautious about what to believe, even while being hopeful. Still, this isn't the real problem. One part, the real question, concerns those wielding the sword and what they do with it.

We call God 'God' because of the miracles He/She performs. Nature itself is a miracle — its abundance, grandeur, its terror, and its beauty. Even with scientists poking up Her sleeves trying to expose Her miracles as astro-bio-tech parlor tricks, there are super-natural occurrences that are still far, far beyond the realm of science to explain away empirically, theoretically, institutionally, or otherwise. But, they can be known — today and since the dawn of time — experientially. In India, those who accomplish this are called Godmen and Godwomen. They exemplify the miraculous power of the Almighty. However, as the parlor trick implies, these things can be faked. Along with miracles and natural phenomenon, our world is privy to false miracles, false science, and false proponents of each as well. What to do? Allow for Time...that's the usual way; in time, everything is revealed. The best way is to be one of 'those who know'; in this case, a Knower of Reality.

For anything to be accomplished there must some *faith* — faith in yourself, in the work, in the knowledge, or faith in the teacher. 'Faith' is not belief. It's more than that. The early 20th Century American healer, Edgar Casey, is said to have described faith as an 'inner knowing'. I would agree with that. My Master used to say in his beginning days, he had no faith in the sacred formulas or the processes, but he had complete faith in the palm leaf manuscripts and the saints who wrote them…and he had pretty good faith in himself. Inner knowing/faith is a subtle, personal experience we must nurture. *"Shraddha and Saburi,"* Shirdi Baba used to say — *faith and patience/practice.* Real faith does not undermine your ability to see and to understand, it enhances it. When you *know,* you have some bearing with which to gauge what is running, the false and the true. The more you know, the better your discrimination, the easier it is to discern the diamond from the glass.

And, in truth, fakers are not really the majority of the lot. Funnily enough, that would go to the category of 'good beginners'. A greater portion fall more into the category of 'experts' than 'embodiments', so-called or otherwise — those who have gained some or a goodly amount of information from books (and other experts), and have the desire to share, and the ability to communicate what they've learned. However, in every endeavor, there is no substitute for direct experience. But, not just experience with the problem(s) or the symptoms — experience with the solutions. A doctor doesn't need to be sick to help a patient. But, to really heal, he needs to do more than mask or band-aid the symptoms. In this light, much of accepted wisdom is neither acceptable nor wise.

There are examples of this 'accepted' silliness in Vaastu, as well, the most prevalent being the existence of a so-called cosmic being known as the *Vaastu Purusha* (the Soul of Vaastu). Commonly, when Vaastu is discussed or taught, a central graphic is the depiction of the *Vaastu Purusha* sitting on his haunches upon a grid. It is said that this cosmic being must be appeased for the inhabitants of a property or home to have success and happiness. Let me illustrate the narrow-mindedness of this. There is a story of a great saint, Tenali Ramakrishna, who while on his way with his family to the court of the king had to stop overnight in a small village. It was late and cold, so they found a small shed to sleep under by the side of the road. During the night there was a big celebration in the village, during which hundreds of animals were slaughtered and offered up to Mother Divine for Her blessing. By the end, the blood of the slaughtered flowed like a river towards the shed where Tenali Ramakrishna, his wife, and son lay. Being a Brahmin (of the priestly caste), he could not touch blood. So, he ran to the site of the ritual, to the temple of Mother Divine, and began to shout at Her in a beautiful way. "Hey, how can you allow this! The animals are your children, too! You are so great. You are our beautiful Mother, the Mother-of-All. Why do you need this terrible horror?!" He kept on like this for a long while. It was very late in the night — a very powerful spiritual time. Suddenly, Mother Divine appeared before him, smiling. "Hey, man! Why are you yelling at me? Fine, it's in a beautiful way, but still, you are yelling. Why?" She said. "So much torture, pain, and awful death…for *You!*" he said. "You are our dearest Heart. We are Your children. Why do You need this?" "Hey, I don't need this," Mother replied. "These children (the participants in the slaughter), they're a little psychiatric. They don't understand Me." "Why don't You stop it?" Tenali Ramakrishna asked. "It's their karma," She replied, "both the people's and the animals. It will come back, don't worry."

Misunderstanding and misinterpretation is, one part, karma — karma coupled with ignorance — which will bear its own karmic fruit. Yet, from one angle, the 'psychiatric patients' were following the ritual instructions. At the same time, they didn't know what they were doing. No one in his right mind would offer such a terrible thing to anyone, Divine or not, if they knew the so-called gift was not wanted or needed. Yet, they were following 'proper' procedural instructions. How did they get those instructions? Whoever gave them, whoever promoted them, perpetuated ignorance and structured more bondage to the Wheel of Karma. What the saints do or can do is one thing.

What is written is another…and in its own beautiful hinting way can be misinterpreted or misused. It takes another saint, who can properly decipher it, who possesses the proper 'pin code', to access and use it properly. Yet, while exemplary proponents of the wisdom appear from time to time, many renderings of the ancient knowledge are commented upon, interpreted, reinterpreted, and propounded by facile students, adept at learning by rote or intellectual analysis, but lacking in the depth of spiritual experience to separate the kernel from the husk.

The understanding of the *Vaastu Purusha* is said to originate with the *Brahma Puranas*, which make up a third of an organized collection of ancient stories from the Vedic wisdom, many of which have to do with the creation of the universe. My Master says, however, that from his personal research, no such being exists. I, of course, have faith in him. So, how did this non-existent 'cosmic' being get into the accepted scriptures, if it doesn't exist? Perhaps, somewhere along the line, a group of middle-class, entrepreneurial pundits got together over chai and thought it was a good idea, a plausible way to increase their income or status. Why didn't the divine souls at the time leap from their huts and smite the blighters? It was their karma. The truth is, over time, knowledge is lost…and over time, there is a revival. It's a spiritual law.

A big part of the reason why the knowledge can't be permanently lost is because it can be directly known, directly experienced. We are living at a time when we can readily see a resurgence of spiritual knowledge in the world. The more fully we plumb the depths of that knowledge and apply it in our daily lives, the more assuredly we will see the bright sun of a new Age not just dawning, but gloriously full…now, in this lifetime…and for a thousand years to come.

CHAPTER 3

THE STRENGTH OF YOUR DIRECTIONS

One of the staples of our life on this blue-green planet is the joy and necessity of accessorizing. In distant isolated villages, in the poorest parts of a country like India, even while working in the rice fields, you will find wonderful women — all extraordinary in their own ways — wearing nose- and earrings, necklaces and bangles. At sunset, stopping by the highway for a bracing shot of chai, you are greeted by the tinkling of ankle bracelets as the women walk past on their way home, children and cow in tow. Think about your own country and countries everywhere. One part, these little things are a luxury. One part, they are required for our wellbeing. In this regard, the most important accessory — one which no woman, child or man should ever be without — is a good pocket compass. It may not be a spiritual law, but it's an important Vaastu asset.

Knowing your place in the scheme of things may not be easy, but knowing where you stand can and should be. If the Five Elements are always in play, then their directional strengths (and weakness) are constantly influencing us — our thoughts and actions — and how the world around us (and especially the folks in the immediate vicinity) respond to us. Learning how the energies play, testing them, and using that knowledge in a beautiful way (no matter what the situation), can make an immediate difference in your life, and one that lasts for the long haul.

You can apply Vaastu wherever you are — at home or the office, at lunch or in a business meeting — everywhere, all the time. As we go more deeply into the details of Vaastu we'll be talking quite a bit in terms of property, structures/buildings, rooms, their configurations, and their energetics. You will naturally think to apply these to your personal property, your home, and the place(s) where you work. But, I want you to keep this point in mind — they are in play *everywhere, all the time.* Do you know where is the natural 'commanding' position/seat at any table? How do you get the best night's sleep — whether at home, in a hotel, or a pup tent in the woods? How do you positively influence any relationship, easily and quickly? One part, wherever you go, the quality of your life experience is a matter of how you face up to what's right in front of you. So, literally, which direction you're facing can make all the difference.

'Direction' implies movement. 'Movement' implies a transfer or transmission of some form of energy. How the natural energies of the Elements display or express themselves is dependent on their placement on a given property, home, etc., in relationship to their natural directional strengths. There are 16 'directions' or divisions of the compass used in Vaastu:

The Four CARDINAL DIRECTIONS
The Four CONVERGENT DIRECTIONS
The Eight SUB-DIRECTIONS

Like the Elements, each direction has its own character, which is either auspicious or inauspicious. When an Element is well-placed, it is naturally strong. However, if an Element's directional strengths are inappropriately used — for example, access to the property, home, etc. is from an inauspicious direction instead of an auspicious one — the natural strength of the Element will be compromised. Energy that flows onto a property from an inauspicious direction dilutes or compromises the positive energetics of the Element associated with that portion of the property, as well as negatively influencing every other Element and the property as a whole. And, conversely, when the positive energy, which holds the integrity of the property, flows out via an inauspicious direction, harmony is diminished according to the depleted, weakened character of the Element situated there.

This is the point where many people begin to get bogged down by what appear to be the growing/layered complexities of Vaastu. It is here that the previous simplicity of the science starts to become variegated because it starts to reveal how, in some cases, a matter of degrees can mean the difference between a positive influence and a negative one. Moreover, a matter of degrees also shifts the intensity as well as the angle of consideration. But, this is also why Vaastu can identify property, building, and room 'defects' and predict the problems running in an inhabitant's life…and offer specific solutions for each and every specific problem.

"God," the saying goes, "is in the details." And, this is one way to know Her. First, grasp the fundamentals — own them in your personal understanding — then apply them and see what the deal is from your direct experience, step-by-step. Yet, the intricacies of Vaastu are such that it is always recommended to get a true Vaastu expert's advice when it comes to dealing with them all. We are talking about your karma after all, your livlihood, your peace and your joy, and that of your family. Certainly, being an 'informed consumer' is a great asset. Still, the point is to be wise.

For example, if a gate or entrance/exit is placed in an inauspicious direction in the area of the property which is the natural home of the Air Element, the inhabitants can experience financial difficulties, legal problems, mental anguish, and emotional upheaval. The play of the directions on the power and influence of the Elements reveal more of the details of exactly what energetic symptoms will manifest in a person's life. That's the deal. Okay, now let's take a closer look at the 16 directions in Vaastu.

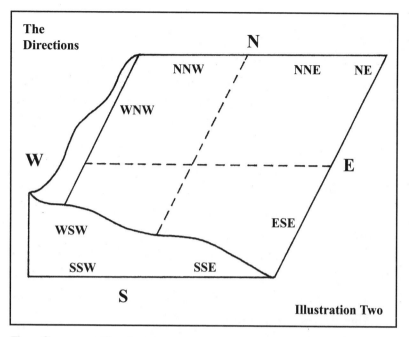

The Directions

N

NNW

NNE

NE

WNW

W

E

WSW

ESE

SSW

SSE

S

Illustration Two

THE CARDINAL DIRECTIONS

These are north, south, east, and west *according to the compass*. Most properties, homes, and offices are built 'directionally' askew, more north-ish than north, and so on. This makes a huge difference when you're plotting your property and seeing how the Elements are situated. When you superimpose a proper cardinal north-south-east-west grid over a map of your property you may find directional cuts or extensions that are detrimental. You also can see how to optimize the energetics of your property to create a kind of Heaven on Earth.

Since the boundaries of most older properties were originally determined by some arbitrary consideration — following the path of a dried riverbed, the ridge of a hill, or the side of a winding road — and current demarcations follow who-knows-what, other than what is already established by deed or law, you'll be super lucky to find a property with boundaries that run along or close to the cardinal directions. But, if you do...buy it!...and keep it! It's a great beginning.

A piece of property is a piece of Earth. Since the Earth is *the* big magnet, the axis of the Earth's magnetism plays an important role in identifying the full extent of the area of your property from which each Element exerts its influence. Magnetic north rules your compass. You can determine a great deal about the potential of a property by how true its eastern and western boundaries follow the point of that little red arrow. The same holds true for the southern boundary (but, of course, running east and west). The northern boundary is a slightly different case, which we'll get into shortly. Suffice it to say, the nearer your property lines follow the cardinal directions the better. To ensure this, we always start by constructing boundary walls at a right angle in the southwest corner.

As it is, most properties are irregularly shaped. The value in following the line of the cardinal directions as closely as you can suggests that a perpendicular, four-sided piece of land would be ideal. The sides don't have to be of equal length; the property can be a square or a rectangle. With every other shape (except a *perfect* circle or a property with a northeast extension), to optimize the Vaastu of a property, you need to reset the property boundaries — aligning them more closely with the north-south and east-west axis — which is easily accomplished by putting up new property barriers, like rows of bushes or compound walls that run around the 'new' parameters of the Vaastu-corrected property. In Ayurveda, India's ancient, natural form of health care, we use the words 'favor' or 'avoid', never 'only' do this or 'only' do that. That is to say, there is some natural leeway for personal considerations. Like that, In Vaastu, up to a 20° tilt off the cardinal axis is allowable, but not more. After this, the energetics can get messy and need a good deal of compensation to rectify sufficiently. After all, who wouldn't rather live in a heaven than in purgatory? Purgatory may not be a hell, but it's close enough.

The north holds and expresses the energetic of Abundance; the east of Wisdom; the south of Power; the west carries the energies of Wellbeing. Since these energies express themselves in this world of duality — both positively and/or negatively — it's practical to optimize their positive qualities in their relationship(s) with the Elements as configured on your property or in your home.

The Four Convergent Directions

Where the north, south, east, and west boundaries meet — north and east in the northeast, east and south in the southeast, south and west in the southwest, and west and north in the northwest — these are called the Convergent directions. Since they mix and hold the energies of two directions, they are super powerful.

The Eight Sub-directions

When you parse the north, south, east, and west boundaries, you find the Sub-directions as follows: north-northeast (NNE), east-northeast (ENE), east-southeast (ESE), south-southeast (SSE), south-southwest (SSW), west-southwest (WSW), west-northwest (WNW), and north-northwest (NNW). These 16 directions are hugely important when considering the strength of what is auspicious and inauspicious regarding a property.

These 16 directions are hugely important when considering the strength of what is auspicious and inauspicious regarding a property.

A Practical Reality Check

Knowing which way is up is, well, a pretty good place to start when considering not only your place in the scheme of things but when considering the lay of the land, especially when it's land you're thinking of purchasing or living on. Firstly, it's important to note that for all practical purposes, there are two North Poles: a true 'geographic' North Pole at the top of the world; and a 'magnetic' North Pole, which is over 1,250 miles away from the true/geographic one. A compass, which is a magnetized instrument, always points toward the magnetic North Pole. However, maps are not oriented to the magnetic North Pole, but to the true North Pole. The angular difference between True North and Magnetic North is called 'declination'. The declination for your spot on the globe varies from 0° to 30° in most populated regions. Additionally, declination values change slightly over time, as the earth's plates shift. The actual value of declination and its annual rate of change are usually indicated on an area map as either an 'easterly' or 'westerly' declination, depending on where you are.

Most compasses have a fixed declination-correction scale to simplify the calculations. However, some have an adjustable declination-correction scale. Remember, in Vaastu, up to a 20° tilt off the Cardinal axis is allowable, but not more. So, your declination is really important. Learning to properly read a map and use a compass are fundamental tools. Don't underestimate this point. It can make a huge difference.

THE FOUR CARDINAL DIRECTIONS

North (N)	**ABUNDANCE**	
East (E)	**WISDOM**	
South (S)	**POWER**	
West (W)	**VITALITY**	

THE FOUR CONVERGENT DIRECTIONS

Northeast (NE)	**ABUNDANCE & WISDOM**
Southeast (SE)	**WISDOM & POWER**
Southwest (SW)	**POWER & VITALITY**
Northwest (NW)	**VITALITY & ABUNDANCE**

THE EIGHT SUB-DIRECTIONS

North-northeast (NNE)	AUSPICIOUS
East-northeast (ENE)	AUSPICIOUS
East-southeast (ESE)	INAUSPICIOUS
South-southeast (SSE)	AUSPICIOUS
South-southwest (SSW)	INAUSPICIOUS
West-southwest (WSW)	INAUSPICIOUS
West-northwest (WNW)	AUSPICIOUS
North-northwest (NNW)	INAUSPICIOUS

As I pointed out earlier, the Earth, Fire, Water, and Air Elements have a home (are well-placed) in a specific quadrant of an office, dwelling, or property: Earth (in the SW), Fire (in the SE), (Water in the NE), and Air (in the NW). And, each Element has its own characteristics and natural energetics. The Earth Element is a huge protection circle: we build compound walls of earthen materials to keep out the errant and negative energies surrounding the property and to circumscribe and hold the integrity of the property itself. One ramification of this is that it's not a good idea to have entrances and exits anywhere in that quadrant — the southwest. A WSW and/or SSW entrance is life-threatening (especially for men); it causes a vast array of health problems. Since the Earth Element protects from negativity, it also carries a 'commanding' energy. If we have entrances and exits in the WSW and/or SSW, that commanding power is compromised, even debilitated. Since the Earth Element is about substance, which implies height and weight, it is the best place for higher ground, and for building the biggest buildings.

Diagonally across from the SW is the NE, the home of the Water Element. Water amplifies and conducts energy. If Earth protects from the negative energies coming onto the property from the S and W in the SW quadrant, it follows that Water amplifies the positive energies of the N and E in the NE quadrant. If 'height and weight' are the physical characteristics functioning to protect from the negativity, then it also follows that open, lower land — ideally with a pond, pool, or fountain — would be optimal in the NE quadrant. And, entrances in the NNE and ENE would also be optimal, to allow the positive energies from those two directions to freely flow on the property.

The SE quadrant is the home of the Fire Element. Here, as in the NW quadrant (the home of the Air Element), one Sub-direction is auspicious and one is inauspicious. For starters, this means access from one Sub-direction is valuable, while another is debilitating. In these two quadrants, the auspicious and inauspicious entrances and exits are also diagonal to each other, i.e. the WNW offers auspicious access, while an ESE access would be inauspicious. Likewise, the SSE access is auspicious, while a NNW access is inauspicious.

As regards auspicious and inauspicious entrances, the auspicious entrances are: north-northeast (NNE), east-northeast (ENE), south-southeast (SSE), and west-northwest (WNW). According to Vaastu, the east-southeast (ESE), south-southwest (SSW), west-southwest (WSW), and north-northwest (NNW) are considered inauspicious accesses, both coming and going. These guidelines also apply to buildings. Even following just these few simple points can change your direct experience of the home, office, and property you inhabit.

THE FOUR QUADRANTS

Northeast (NE)	**ABUNDANCE & WISDOM (WATER)**
Southeast (SE)	**WISDOM & POWER (FIRE)**
Southwest (SW)	**POWER & VITALITY (EARTH)**
Northwest (NW)	**VITALITY & ABUNDANCE (AIR)**

Whenever considering a property, first consider the alignment of the boundaries according to the Cardinal directions on your compass. You can do this by superimposing a Cardinal grid over a drawing of the property, making the proper adjustment for your declination. This visual aid is a tool to help you more easily see the largest 'ideal' shape (a square or rectangle) within the existing property.

Unless the property is a perfect square or rectangle, the first thing you will notice is that there are extensions to the property at various locations. Now, properly place the Elements on the grid. If an existing property runs outside the largest ideal boundaries, which it naturally will — or if it cuts inside those boundaries in one direction or another — you need to adjust the actual physical boundaries of your property accordingly. When making such adjustments, it's important to consider the sub-directional points regarding auspicious and inauspicious access. Wherever a property extends, it extends the influence of the Element situated there and factors in the sub-directional strength as well. According to Vaastu, the underlying premise in this regard is how Nature works in this Age — the *Kaliyuga*, as it's called, the Age of Ignorance — and the spiritual laws that guide the evolution of our souls as well as the practical considerations of day-to-day life at this time in the history of mankind. Accordingly, it is necessary is to put primary value on Wisdom (the east) and Abundance (the north). Therefore, the highest priority is given to the NE and, in turn, the east and north. Many traditionalists continue to promote the east as the highest priority, but this is past-Age wisdom. Now, Abundance is equally required, and is needed as a support for Wisdom. In this Age, they go hand-in-hand. Many saints and seers have noted that in the past, wealth has been equally swayed by good or bad intent. We see this every day. In the hands of selfish people, wealth has given them the means, the energy, and access to do terrible things. Now, as we move into a new Age, wealth in the hands of those with more spiritual intent is a requirement for fulfillment of an individual's, a community's, and humankind's highest ideals; and the spiritual laws in play support this. Where, in Ages past, an individual would have to go through and overcome almost insurmountable trials just to reach a place where spiritual realization was actively promoted and won, now (in part) it's a matter of scheduling the time and swiping a Visa card. Like that, when it comes to building your own personal heaven, the only real obstacles are time and money. So, when deciding on the best configuration of an existing property, keep in mind these points.

OPTIMAL EXTENSIONS

Northeast (NE) **ABUNDANCE & WISDOM** (WATER)

North-northeast (NNE) **ABUNDANCE & WISDOM** (WATER) AUSPICIOUS

East-northeast (ENE) **Abundance & Wisdom** (Water) AUSPICIOUS

OPTIONAL: South-southeast (SSE) **WISDOM & POWER** (FIRE) AUSPICIOUS

OPTIONAL: West-northwest (WNW) **VITALITY & ABUNDANCE** (AIR) AUSPICIOUS

If the existing property extends to the NNW, ESE, SSW, SW, or WSW, you have to close it off and never...never...use those portions of the property (sorry, no 'favor' or 'avoid' here — I told you there were exceptions).

THE BEST EXCEPTION

The best property has a NE extension, with greater open space and lower typography than the rest of the property. If 'height' and 'weight' in the SW is a guiding rule, then lower, open space to the north and east follows. The more open and unencumbered the space to the north and east, the greater ease of access and flow for the energies of Abundance and Wisdom. It's possible to have the downward slope fan out from the SW to include the NW and the SE, but even then the lowest part of the property should be in the NE.

SOME POINTS ON ABUNDANCE

'Abundance' is not just about money, but money is a huge energy when it comes to facilitating the experience of abundance. There is an old saying, "No man thinks of God on an empty stomach." Money is not a luxury; it is a means of exchange. It allows for both the necessities of life to be in place as well as facilitates the expansion of one's experience in innumerable ways. When someone's necessities are secured and in place, he can turn his attention to 'more' — more things, more knowledge, more relationships/exchanges, more variety of material, intellectual, heartful, and spiritual experiences. Money facilitates the expansion of our horizons. When the qualities of the north direction are allowed to express themselves fully and positively, almost anything is possible.

SOME POINTS ON WISDOM

Whether you have faith in what or who you call a Higher/Highest Power, Spirit, God, or Being, what you are experiencing and expressing is the Divine quality of Life's breadth and depth. Knowledge of This is inspiring. Understanding This brings peace. Knowledge and Understanding coupled with Direct Experience brings Wisdom. Wisdom is the (super)natural consequence of the expansion of one's own direct experience of the depth and breadth of life, including the miraculous. Expansion...knowing more...seeing more...understanding more...experiencing more (and more deeply)...these are the expressed-nature of the Divine within this realm of the Five Elements. The east — home of the sun, from where its healing, life-sustaining, ever-growing light and *prana* (the Life Force) washes over us each day — is the energetic bearer of Wisdom.

SOME POINTS ON POWER

My Master once drew a 'chart' of the Divine. At the top was the single word, 'Divine'. Below that he wrote, 'Divine Positive' and 'Divine Negative'. Below 'Divine Positive' he wrote, 'Manifest Positive'. Below 'Divine Negative' he wrote, 'Used Negative'. We've all read stories of the celestial battles between the gods and the demons. They appear in almost all ancient literature. And, the stories primarily seem to be about — or at least include — a struggle for power. What is the nature of this…the inner mechanisms? The underlying source is clearly the Divine. Positive and negative, therefore, both have the spark of the Divine in them. And so, 'Power' is inherent; but, it is also expressed — manifest and used. Thus, it is worthwhile to manifest the positive channels of power and protect against the misuses, or negative uses of it. The south is the directional home of Power. So, we build high, and from this elevated position (with the magnetic power of the Earth and the transformative power of the Fire and the vital energy of the Air) — all within the protection of compound walls — we open ourselves to the expansive energies of Abundance and Wisdom (amplified by the optimal placement and use of the Water Element in the NE). In this way, we construct a firm foundation for commanding on life in a beautiful way, for living life masterfully.

SOME POINTS ON VITALITY

According to the ancient wisdom, 'Vitality', as in the case of the character of the west in Vaastu, directly inspires 'longevity' and 'industriousness'. This is where the age-old idea/expression, 'An active life is a healthy life,' comes from. Physical and mental activity/stimulation play a big part in creating and maintaining optimal health. In Vaastu, 'longevity' is strongly linked to the WSW and 'industriousness' is linked to the WNW. The WSW is associated

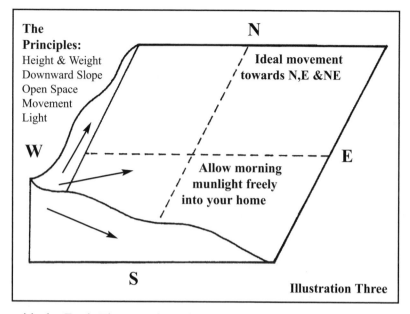

The Principles:
Height & Weight
Downward Slope
Open Space
Movement
Light

N

Ideal movement towards N,E &NE

W

Allow morning munlight freely into your home

E

S

Illustration Three

with the Earth Element; thus, the quality of 'longevity'. The WNW is associated with the Air Element; thus, the quality of active progress or 'industriousness'. In Vedic astrology, it is said that, "Life is lived through relationships": our relationship with our environment (including the planets and the stars), with other souls, and with our 'self' — our own inner worlds (the mind-body connection). 'Relationships' imply 'connection' and, to some degree or another, 'intimacy'. Since we also work through some of our karma (present and past-life exchanges of energy) in this life, vitality, longevity, and industriousness help us experience and resolve a large quantity of our karmas and afford us the best opportunity for the highest possible quality of life. Change your Vaastu and you change your karma. That's a spiritual law — in every Age — but, now, more than ever, it's a real necessity if our intent is to bring heaven on earth, for ourselves, our families and friends, and for the world.

CHAPTER 4

THE PRINCIPLES IN PRACTICE

We have touched on the principles in relationship to the Elements, their directional strengths, and their characters. Vaastu's main principles are the connective tissue of this beautiful, ancient body of work. They offer nutritive insight to the diagnosis of the health (or lack of it) for an existing property, home, or workplace. Moreover, they make up the blueprint for rectifying any defect and transforming your home and office into a paradise.

THE MAIN PRINCIPLES
HEIGHT & WEIGHT
DOWNWARD SLOPE
OPEN SPACE & LIGHT
MOVEMENT

HEIGHT & WEIGHT

Height and weight offer both protection and a commanding position. As mentioned earlier, 'height and weight' imply the Earth Element, whose character is magnetic, nurturing, organizing, powerful, and strong. Thus, the highest elevation on a property is best situated in the SW quadrant of a property (the home of the Earth Element). It is also a great Vaastu point to have your property butting against a hill or mountain in the SW. It offers huge protection power.

Not only should your property be higher in the SW, but this is the best place to build your home — and all large buildings. Even the buildings themselves should have the highest portion/room(s) in the SW, if possible. If the house is in any way tiered, it should begin with the greatest height in the SW. Since greater 'height/and/weight' in the south and west is a good thing, planting tall trees, high hedges, and or thicker, higher compound walls in these directions are plus points.

DOWNWARD SLOPE

'Height and Weight' in one direction implies less height and more openness in the other directions. An ideal property has a downward slope to the north, east, and northeast. Even if it's only a few inches, a downward slope helps to perpetuate the inherent prowess and strength of all that is raised from behind and adds to support the integration and expression of all that lies before it.

OPEN SPACE & LIGHT

Since, rightfully so, in Vaastu the greatest priority is given to the qualities of Abundance and Wisdom that the NE confers, a property should offer as much unencumbered access to those energetics as possible. The greater the open space to the NE (especially), and to the N and E, the better the Vaastu. Since that area is the home of the Water Element (which amplifies) and the directional convergence of the energetics of Abundance and Wisdom, besides the compound walls and entrances/exits, the only 'improvement' to the property there should be a pond, pool, or fountain. At Sri Sai Kaleshwara's ashram in Penukonda, he has made a beautiful, expansive, peaceful garden where students sit to meditate, walk, and often gather for his talks. Also, in the NE corner is a wonderful fountain, which is lit at night.

BRINGING IN THE LIGHT

As I mentioned, Vedic astrology is called 'Jyotish', which means 'light' — it shines light on the path of the soul so that we are illumined and have greater ease to make better choices. Whereas, in the dark, whatever is present is unseen or in shadows and, thus, become obstacles along our path. Bringing in the light changes our direct experience — what was once unseen now becomes simply another opportunity for enjoyment, stimulation, and upliftment. This is the nature of light.

Dawn's early light is powerfully healing — physically, emotionally, and spiritually. It carries the life force, awakening all of nature as it grows, and stirs the impulse of Wisdom within us. As much access as possible to this light is a super Vaastu point. Thus, open space is an important requirement. Furthermore, large windows and unimpeded views, which allow the greatest amount of morning light into one's home or office, is a top priority.

Many believe that in our hemisphere it is a practical architectural imperative to have as much light as possible coming in from the south, as this direction allows for the longest amount of sunlight to shine in because of the sun's trajectory. Fine. This is understandable. But, this is a consideration of *quantity*. We must also consider *quality*. Nothing in life stays static; and sunlight is no exception. More than its apparent movement across the sky, the energetics of the sun's light also takes on different qualities as it makes its way across the sky. For example, the afternoon light is sharp and burning; whereas the morning's light is warming, soothing and nurturing. Recognizing and using the natural energetics of life leads us to living and realizing the supernatural, divine energetics of life as well. The morning's light purifies one's inner spaces — those inside your home and those inside yourself.

MOVEMENT

Can you guess which way is optimal for movement on a property or in a home? Which direction(s) are most conducive for the flow of energy...from your side, the standpoint of the inhabitant? Okay, that last bit should have been enough of a hint. Ideally, the *majority* of your movements should be, one, towards the NE, and, two, towards the N and E. If you remember back to the Sub-directions, the auspicious entrance/exits are: NNE, ENE, SSE, and WNW, with the optimal entrances/exits in the NNE and ENE. Moving towards the energetics of Abundance and Wisdom enhances the flow of these divine energies in your life. You take them in with each breath. Of course, practical logistics dictate that some movement in other directions is required. But, the point remains: the *majority* of movement is best directed to the NE, N, and E. On a property, in a traditional Indian home built according to Vaastu, they place water tanks on top of the home in the SW corner so the majority of the water also runs towards the north, east, and northeast (note: enclosed water is not the same as open water). Like that, if you have running water channels — natural streams or manmade ones — the water should optimally flow NE, N, and E.

Connecting The Main Principles

With height and weight in the SW, a downward slope to the NE, N, and E, and more open space in the NE, N, and E, and with the home and property configured in such a way as to allow for the majority of movement to the NE, N, and E, you have the makings of a tremendously powerful and supportive environment…and a powerfully vital and abundant life — one filled with wisdom and grace.

Even a cave can be found and 'remodeled' with good Vaastu in mind. But, since modern building materials are more plastic and easily turned to our personal preferences and uses, the possibilities these days are enormous. As you come to know and own these Vaastu points on the Elements, the directions, the main principles, and their interconnectedness, you will start to recognize the amazing influence your environment actually has on your life — for good or ill — and what changes you can make to support your hopes and dreams and desires, and empower your deepest longings so that they actually manifest in your life. Vaastu is a powerful tool to help you know who you truly are and what your highest purpose is here on this planet. And that, dear hearts, truly does make all the difference.

CHAPTER 5

YOU & VAASTU — APPLYING THE PRACTICE

The fundamentals may indeed bring grace and wisdom, but joy lies in the details. Attention to detail also brings illumination. Vaastu defects display certain symptoms in the lives of the inhabitants. So does good Vaastu. Of course, if all things were equal, we'd each build the coolest, biggest, and most spiritual palace we could imagine. The truth is, that's exactly what we've done. We live and build and create our 'world' according to our perception. The Vaastu of the place where you now live reflects your personal karma — 'karma' meaning (the natural) reaction to the actions *you've* created through the illusion that is covering you.

That is to say, each of us lives in our own world, a world similar to everyone else's, yet unique...because of our personal actions/ reactions (our karma), motivated by our perception as it unfolded in the past and as it unfolds in the present. Thus, in our world we have authority to act and react, one part, impelled by the pressures exerted upon us by our past actions and, from another angle, by how we react to the world based on how it reflects back to us our perception of it. We have such authority because the Divine in us (and in our worlds) has made this pact of uniqueness with us; thus, we are responsible for 'our world'. This, then, is the source of 'the illusion' that covers us: our individual worlds are similar yet unique; and so, personal authority is there, but because the Divine in all is also expressed as the inherent similarity between all existing 'worlds', we are not, in fact, autonomous. Life is lived through relationships: relationship with our environment, with other souls, and with our inner self. I don't wake up and wonder what I'm to do in Tom's world, today, or in anyone else's. I wake up wondering about *my* world, my place in it, and what it has is store for me. But, it is imperative that I take others into consideration as well.

In direct relationship with the Divine, we live by permission. That's the deal. However, until we realize the truth of our own divinity, even our true sense of authority is compromised — one part, because of the illusion of the inherent (and apparent) lack of autonomy; and, one part, because of our ignorance of the particulars (our personal actions/reactions and perception) during our past lives. Until we realize the truth of our own divinity, we live under the illusion of compromise and lack. Our personal perception, as structured and motivated by our karma (past and present), is one of the most powerful single ingredients in our lives.

Since the Divine exists and is every thing and everywhere (as well as within us), our environment/world and our karma are intimately connected. The environment — the energetics of nature — is the realm of Vaastu. To a huge extent, your Vaastu energetically supports your karma. That's actually why you live in the place and under the physical circumstances you do. To better understand the problems in your life, look to your Vaastu. It is a barometer of your present and your future. 80% of your problems can be identified right there. Again, change your Vaastu and you change your life.

PRINCIPLE DEFECTS

If you have Height and Weight in the NE of your property, according to the principles of Vaastu, it doesn't mean you rotate the 'natural' Element placement and put 'the home of the Earth Element' there. It means the natural energetics of the NE — of Abundance and Wisdom — are blocked and gravely compromised. If you have a NNW (inauspicious) entrance, which is intimately connected with the quality of the north's Abundance as well as the NW quadrant (the home of the Air Element), financial difficulties will occur, so will legal problems. 'Inauspicious' Air means things move too quickly — they come and go, and too fast for comfort — and when things move too quickly, confusion arises. Conversely, air can be stale or stuck, creating a lack of movement or natural, invigorating flow. Thus, financial difficulties and legal problems *naturally* result from either condition.

If you have the greatest Height and Weight in the SE (the home of the Fire Element)…well, what happens when you put too much wood on the fire? It smothers. Fire is transformational; it's nurturing, warm, and welcoming. What happens when this energy is 'smothered'? Looking at it from another angle, since 'female' energy is deeply connected to the energetics of Fire Element, how do you think this defect would manifest via the mind, body, and emotions, especially in women? What is the experience when a woman's nurturing warmth is 'snuffed out' (that is to say, buried/sublimated deep within)? Passion/inner fire, warmth, and by extension joyous expression — both in the woman and, by extension, in her children and in her spouse/mate — are deeply compromised (and can be for a long, long time) — unless the woman's natural, intimate, and balanced connection to the Fire is realigned. And, if the home of the Fire Element is otherwise compromised — for example, it's the lowest, most open part of the property — tempers flare; instead of just cooking our food, we 'cook' the family, energetically speaking. Thus, proper placement and support for the Fire Element is also key to success in relationships, in terms of their growth and wellbeing. Ideally, then, when the use of fire is called for (such as in cooking), it's best done in the SE quadrant; and, since, N and E are the auspicious directions to face in order to receive/gain the beautiful, divine 'openness' of Abundance, Wisdom, and Light, cooking — not 'prepping', but cooking (using the fire/heat) — is best done while facing N and E.

If you have open space and a downward slope to the SW, what happens? Since, one part, height and weight provide protection against negativity, your energetic protection is gone; the energetics of longevity, vitality, and power are also gravely compromised. And, since 'male' energy is strongly influenced there, what do you think a man's physical health and wellbeing will be as a result? Such a Vaastu defect is life threatening. If you have open space and a downward slope to the S and W (especially to the SW), change it...or sell it!

Water amplifies. Properly placed in the NE quadrant, it increases the positive expression of the Divine energetics of Abundance, Wisdom, and Light. If the energetics of the Divine are blocked there — by tall trees, buildings, high ground and/or an upward slope (all Earth), or the Water Element is poorly placed (in another area, for example) — not only do you *not* enjoy the flow or added natural amplification of these beautiful NE characteristics into your life, but the poorly placed Water Element will amplify the NE defect to some extent, which can be hugely damaging to everyone living on the property.

While all the major defects presented above are crucial and must be remedied, if at all possible, Vaastu still gives top priority to the N, E, and NE. So, you must add to the 'Elemental' defects, the very important consideration of directional defects — inauspicious entrances/exits, a lack of open access and auspicious flow/movement to the NNE, NE, and ENE, as examples — and, well, you can see the plethora of defects insidiously mounting. My Master says never...never...compromise with Vaastu. Take that as another golden statement.

AN OUNCE OF PREVENTION AND/OR A POUND OF CURE

When looking at a property, home, or office, consider the Vaastu. If you see major defects, so sorry...it's better to move on. Major defects have tendrils that multiply and multiply as you get deeper and deeper into the minutia, and are farther-reaching than you can imagine at a single glance...or even after two or three. Interestingly, most of us look to considerations such as immediate financial concerns (what we think we can 'afford') and visual embellishments (always having wanted that blanched wood/beach house 'look', with the cedar shingles), along with 'wellness' (it's a 'nice' neighborhood near good schools) and 'ease' (it's close to shopping, movies, and work) and consider these points crucial, although in truth they are peripheral. What is the *actual* cost of a new, reasonably priced, Tudor-style 3-Br, 2-bath, on 4 acres, estate if it perpetuates (or God forbid, creates) a dysfunctional family? Is it worth buying a place — or renting for that matter — just because down the hill to the SW there's a beautiful view of the bay? In such an 'idyllic' scenario, what is the actual value, esthetics aside, of French doors and windows, if as a selling point they 'enhance' the opportunity for life-threatening disease, chronic illness, and personal (and residual) on-going pain and suffering? Honestly, none.

Of course, in most Western urban and suburban areas, finding a location with excellent or even primarily good Vaastu is pretty tough. The world is simply built wrong. Cultural bias aside, Vaastu is not an 'Indian' thing; it's Nature's thing. Not having known about Vaastu *is* certainly an excuse, even a good one. But, what good are excuses, especially if you're betting your life and the lives of your family on them? Honestly...

This Age is clearly dominated by negativity. None of us has to go out of his way to be confronted by trials and tribulations. We find them without any effort — and/or they find us — pretty much each and every day. Finding happiness and peace, on the other hand, is pretty tough, even if we seek it whole-heartedly. Even if it comes without being sought after, the common experience is it doesn't last. We plan, scheme, attempt to control, all in the pursuit of happiness. Yet, what is our success rate? It's not a big stretch to agree on this point: the energetics of the world today is 75% negative and 25% positive. That's got to — and can — change. Vaastu is a huge tool for this, one capable of changing the quality of Life as we now know it, for the better.

A case in point: my Master's ashram in Penukonda, Andhra Pradesh, started as a single, one-room, thatched-roofed hut, constructed with Vaastu in mind. By his account, in this life, he started his sojourn there in the 1990s as a single man in his 20s. Within the last few years, the ashram has grown from those humble beginnings — a simple hut in the forest — to include more than 150 Western-standard apartments, over 10 acres of beautiful grounds and improvements, including floral gardens, a 30-foot fountain, a beautiful free-standing Samadhi shrine (to enclose his remains), and the magnificent 2-story temple to his Master, Shirdi Sai Baba and (on the second floor) to 'the Big Boss', Jesus…and it's still growing. It is, in effect, a paradise — spiritually, materially, and esthetically — and all of it is built according to Vaastu. Fine, he is a singular individual, and this extraordinary place is but a singular instance. Yet, in truth, it is a research and development laboratory for Vaastu in this day and Age — a solid, proven, in-this-world example of the power of Vaastu. I'm telling you, change your Vaastu and you change your life.

BUILDING A NEW AGE ONE BRICK AT A TIME

We are intimately connected to our environment and to each other. We use the creative impulse, for better or worse, based on our perception. We attempt to command our environment and others from our own sense of personal authority and power. But, because our perception lacks (to whatever degree) a substantive, direct, conscious connection to our inherent, universal, divine source, the results in our individual world — and all the individual worlds we touch — more often than not border on disastrous. We have little or no depth of understanding of the laws of nature governing the warp and woof of our existence. Even when we gain some understanding of the workings of nature, we do not apply it from the standpoint of real wisdom...because we do not yet own that wisdom; we apply it from a state of ignorance — from a position of 'lack' — and do so in the name of an authority that is wrapped in and colored by our own personal illusion. Thus, we believe that the world/environment must conform to our personal perception of it, instead of doing all that we can to change, evolve, and broaden/deepen our perception to align with the universal truths expressed in Nature. How to change that, since logically we must or perish? This is the realm of human spirituality, which encompasses not only the so-called, invisible esoterica of our inner worlds, but also (forgive me) the meat and potatoes of everyday life on this planet.

To do this, we must change our karma and our perception. Once, a young shaman asked me if it wasn't an aberration of the natural order of things to 'change someone's karma'. But, if the world and its flux is a part of the Divine Plan, wouldn't changing one's karma for the better also be a Divine truth and a gift, a boon afforded us, a shedding of Divine grace and compassion, and thus of 'natural' causes, albeit extraordinary? Could anyone even rationally consider such grace and compassion beyond the capacity of the Divine? Quantum leaps are part of the natural order of things. A saint is a part of the natural order, just as the 'common' man is just as miracles are. 'Becoming' is not the sole order of things; 'Being', in fact, is a truer — that is to say, a deeper, more ubiquitous — truth. 'Awakening' (from the thick clouds of Ignorance/Illusion) is a temporary stage; whereas being 'Awake' (spiritually, divinely Illumined) is more of the nature of a practical immortality, because of its direct, conscious channel to the Divine Source in and of all.

We have been given such boons…in the past and present living embodiments of Divine Wisdom walking among us from Age to Age, and in the oral and written expositions of the wisdom they've left to guide us along the path of our souls. Vaastu is an integral part of this wholly natural and divine guidance. The time has come — now, at the turn of the Age — for the true and practical, spiritual mastery of Life.

CHAPTER 6

BAD VAASTU — A PRECAUTIONARY TALE

Near the start of this book I made the statement that, in terms of Vaastu, my life was my proof…and postulated that it's the same for each of us. Look back at your residences and their energetic configurations and you'll see a blueprint for the play of karma in your life. Your Vaastu *supports* your karma and your karma leads you to Vaastu that reflects it. This is one of the underlying, motivating factors for changing your Vaastu: to change your karma in a beautiful way. In so doing, you open yourself up to enormous possibilities for spiritual — and material — growth. Since such a profound change quickens your pace along the path of your soul, there's no longer any need to entertain the premise that awakening to, realizing and living your own personal spiritual mastery needs to take years, decades, or lifetimes. Identifying where you are is valuable; knowing where you're going is inspiring; but what I'd like to address at this point are some of the signposts along the way and what we can do with them to enhance our journey.

Like everything in this world of duality, every shade of that which we perceive as good and bad is a viable possibility within the broad strokes of our personal life experiences. In this Age, when the bad greatly outweighs the good, it's extremely important not to nurture the negative — there's already enough to go around. But, it's also truly unenlightened to ignore it.

This first point — not nurturing the negativity — may seem obvious, but for most of us it's very difficult, in practice. Why would that be, especially since it seems like it ought to be a primary consideration in an Age dominated by negativity? One part, in our communal mindset, 'not nurturing negativity' takes a back seat to the active pursuit of happiness. Yet, even with all the techniques and tools at our disposal, the common experience is: being happy is a big challenge. We have to work at it.

Even being consistently positive in our thoughts, words, and actions is rare — something many of us consider to be an inherent characteristic of being happy, and often one we're either 'born with' or is a matter of luck. However, since the so-called lucky and the silver-spooned seem very much in the minority, the rest of us pre-suppose that we can win 'being happy' through diligent hard work...since it is a wonderful trait worth mastering. One pitfall here, of course, is that many of us have problems with things we have to diligently practice, especially when they're etheric in nature and the process comes with no guarantee of success; and so, as a natural part of the pursuit, along the way we need regular motivation (usually from an outside source/expert), and periodic positive reiteration (of our goal and our worthiness to reach it) — as well as periodic (and, hopefully, positive) distraction for the sake of variety — even when our goal is something both 'good for us' *and* something we 'truly want'. Still, to date, for most of us owning the state of 'being happy' remains elusive, its active ingredients ever-changing — sometimes more material, sometimes a dash more emotional, sometimes bordering on soulful, while as often as not the mind steps in and questions the present status, anyway...and calls for a new alignment of the parameters altogether. The thing is, the *pursuit* of happiness is a dense illusion within the Illusion, but happiness is not...joy is not...bliss is not; they are, in fact, natural *by-products*...*symptoms* of natural living, of living in accord with nature. If and as we address the nature directly, we realize the natural by-products of that intimate relationship/union *automatically*.

In this light, 'not nurturing the negativity' is a very direct way of manifesting peace and joy in an Age whose character is predominantly negative. To this, add *not minding* — developing an 'adjusting' nature, as my Master calls it — which means structuring a sweet yet commanding flexibility in our character, so that our pursuits in life are not a matter of running after expectations, anticipating results, and/or being bound within the limits of our attachments to the process and the goals we set for ourselves (and our lives) under those constraints.

A good percentage of what we do in our daily life is done out of habit, including living by expectation and relating to others/the world in the context of our desires as well as our attachments. These habits create boundaries, limits the channels through which our energy is expressed and through which we receive and exchange energy with others. In the Vedic tradition, it is understood that you can change a habit in 41 days and create a new energetic 'state' within 101 days. The extent to which the change is complete is, one part, a matter of regular, daily use of the tools for change — such as *sadhana* (spiritual practices) — and following the *dikshas* (guidelines/parameters), which help the new energy be digested and the new stage held/maintained. In spiritual terms, 'diligent' practice simply means doing it over and over again *with intent* (of doing it well and following the guidelines) until we get really good at it.

For many on the spiritual path, the second part of the quandary — not ignoring negativity — is as great or perhaps an even greater challenge. In truth, focusing solely on the positive does not overcome negativity; it isolates us from gaining true mastery over the realities of this existence, whether we pretend/believe they're just an illusion or not. No matter how many soothing pastel walls you surround yourself with…no matter how much sweet music wafts through your halls…nor how much purely *sattvic* food you ingest…you cannot delete negativity. In this world, it's important to *understand* the negative and the positive — their mechanics — in order to grasp the Divine and hold onto it.

In *Ayurveda* (India's natural form of health care), it is said that to feel fulfilled you need to ingest/experience all six tastes life offers — sweet, sour, salty, bitter, pungent, and astringent. Each is powerfully medicinal when used well. It is not required to dive into one or the other for a prolonged time; in fact, it's not recommended. Variety is the spice of life. Filling your life only with sweet things will eventually make you lethargic and ultimately inflexible. A life of bitterness eventually makes you dry and brittle — physically, emotionally, mentally, and spiritually. Too pungent, and you burn up from the inside, making yourself and your life (especially your relationships with others) dry and ashen. There is a better way. In the hands of a master chef, a dash of this or that makes a scrumptious meal. When it comes to sustenance, vitality, longevity, and ultimately fulfillment — in every aspect of life — one part, it's a matter of proper seasoning.

With Vaastu, we can gauge how well we've apportioned the karmic, energetic 'seasoning' in our life, and where we can practically adjust the recipe more to our enlightened tastes. Here are some samples worth considering.

Too Much & Too Little

If you follow the main principles of Vaastu, it's easy to surmise that if and when you see the opposite of good Vaastu, it's a clear indication of bad Vaastu. For example, if it's best to have height and weight in the southwest and the largest amount of open space in the northeast, then height and weight in the northeast and more open space in the southwest are big Vaastu defects — the worst, in fact. **Height and weight in the northeast** will literally ruin your life. Financial losses, relationship problems, and childhood diseases, all result from this life-threatening defect. You'll have to work 100 times harder to win success at your job than you would if this configuration of your property (and/or in your home) was reversed. If not, you will also find yourself with more enemies in your life. They will come in surprising ways and, as often as not, unannounced. If you have the greatest **height mainly in the north**, it's extremely likely you'll go broke, lose your reputation, and generally be miserable. And, when **greater height and weight occur in the east**, life will be stressful, and you'll be consistently and extremely irritable. Even if you make money (which will be a struggle), you'll also incur debt. On top of all that, it's a pretty harsh life risk, especially for men.

When there's **greater height and weight in the northwest**, along with strong financial difficulties, you'll experience mental instability, and your relationships will be a battle. And, more than likely, you'll lose your home/property to boot. With height and weight dominating in the southeast of your property (outside is not a real problem, but *on* your property is), accidents become a regular occurrence. The same thing goes for health and relationship problems. On top of all that, with or without your notice, you'll actually experience a depletion of your willpower.

If you have a **downward slope to the southwest**, it's a real life risk and should be avoided at all costs. The list of 'symptoms' is harrowing: accidents, financial ruin, illness, anger/fighting, jealousy, mistrust, worry, depression, immoral behavior, and even unnatural deaths (such as suicide and murder), all commonly result. A southern downward slope causes chronic illness, heartbreak, confusion, depression, addictions, and stirs up your enemies. A southeast downward slope brings fires, arguments, heart attacks, accidents, robberies, and long-term illnesses, especially for women. A **downward slope to the west** creates failure in all your endeavors. Crazy things will start happening in your life, including the strong pressure to leave everything behind and run. A **downward slope to the north-**

west creates legal problems, loss of your standing in the community (including defamation of character), and usually results in loss of your property as well. It's also very hurtful to personal relationships.

Not following the principles of Vaastu doesn't simply mean there is lack of good, positive, energetic support for one angle or another in your life. It means you can really damage your whole life...and the lives of those around you, your near-and-dear ones, your associates, and your community. Since your Vaastu supports your karma, bad Vaastu supports and nurtures bad karma. It brings it to you. Change your Vaastu and you change your life.

'Too much' and/or 'too little' do not just apply to Height and Weight, Open Space, Movement, and/or Downward Slope. Ideally, you want the boundaries of your property to follow the Cardinal   directions as closely as possible. If the **orientation of your property is greater than 20° off True North**, that's bad Vaastu. You can re-orient your property boundaries by building new compound walls. Remember, the most ideal shape for a property is four-sided (rectangle or square) and, whenever possible, with the property extended to the northeast. However, since most of us don't have a strictly four-sided property shape and probably find it hard to wrap our heads (specifically our sense of territorial ownership) around the idea of cutting off and *never* using a piece of the property we paid good money for, we do need to wrap our heads around this: don't ignore the negative...and accentuate/enhance the positive...or your life *will* crash. By walling off bad Vaastu portions of your property you can extend and enhance the good Vaastu effects of the auspicious areas.

Remember, inches count. It doesn't have to be yards. But, never forget, just like good Vaastu, the energetics of bad Vaastu are cumulative. Anything you can do to mitigate the negative points helps. The more you do, the better — especially if you do it in such a way as to actually further enhance the positive points. You can never make your Vaastu 'too' good. Though in this world of duality there must be some room for the negativity!

So, don't try to get too tricky. It can backfire. I know a couple who tried to make a 'positive' extension in the middle of the eastern side of their property — right in the center along the border line — by walling off the ENE and the ESE thirds along their eastern property line. Without the *exact* declination — how far east or west off True North their actually property line runs — they simply calculated the center point mathematically and proceeded from there.

Although an extension to the east brings 'noble' qualities to the life, this 'positive' extension actually created a cut in the northeast, which in effect blocks happiness and success in the life. They subsequently experienced financial losses and substantive damage to their reputation. Furthermore, he developed a heart condition. So, keep it simple. Extensions are a super-tricky subject. Best rule of thumb: don't mess with the east or north, except to enhance them. And, always consult a certified Vaastu expert. You'll be grateful for it — now and later.

MORE POINTS TO PONDER

CLOSURE

If at all possible, never have a structure within the property butt up against your property line or compound wall. We know that a structure in the SW quadrant is most ideal — the NW and SE are tied for second, while a structure in the NE is a no-no. But, **a house or garage butting up against a compound wall in the SW** creates a *closure,* which blocks the natural, positive energy and, thus, also brings accidents and unnatural deaths, financial loss, depression, enemies, and failure. Always leave or create some space between any structure and the property enclosure. Otherwise, you're setting yourself up for a fall.

PROPER PLACEMENT OF ENTRANCES/EXITS

You should always enter/exit your property *directly* facing the Cardinal directions according to the compass, not the property line or street angle — and, again, only via auspicious entrances/exits. Think about this point...enter/exit your property directly facing the Cardinal directions *according to the compass*, not the property line or street angle. I know, it sounds like a pain: if your property wall isn't aligned with the Cardinal directions according to the compass, then to align the gate/entryway you've got to make/build a 'jog' in the wall to create the proper alignment. Well, yes. That's correct. And, yes, it's worth the trouble...*really* worth it. Your entrances/exits are a focal point for energy exchange between your property and the surrounding community. Therefore, making sure this point is also well taken care of ensures and enhances a positive, auspicious exchange.

STREET FOCUS

When a street intersects or dead ends at your property it vastly increases the energy of the direction from which it comes. Therefore, a street focus should only occur in the NNE, ENE, SSE, or WNW of your property. Otherwise, it needs to be avoided or fixed.

If, for example, a street heads towards your property but veers parallel to it when it comes near, you have to calculate the closest distance it comes to your property to gauge whether it is indeed a street focus or not. If it's within 20 feet of your property, it's a street focus; farther, and it's not. If it's within 20 feet, you have to determine the angle it would hit your property if it didn't veer off. That's the direction/sub-direction you have to consider. In this way, you can determine whether it's an auspicious or inauspicious street focus.

You can remedy an inauspicious street focus by creating an

intervening property. You can do this by getting permission to construct (and, of course, paying for) a city-owned median and/or city-owned sidewalks. If this option isn't possible, you can create an intervening property by walling off and selling that 'new' property to someone else or donating it to the city. In Penukonda, for example, where the ashram had an inauspicious NNW street focus, my Master walled off the property and built a small temple there, which he donated to the village. Here in the West, I suppose we wouldn't build a temple, but we could donate the new property to the city to be used as a small park or simply a 'natural' area. Just make sure that, in the end, the portion you sell/donate doesn't compromise the Vaastu of your 'new' property by making an inauspicious cut or extension. Do it in such a way that it actually enhances your property's Vaastu.

WATER ON OR NEAR YOUR PROPERTY

Since the home of the Water Element is in the NE quadrant, water — such as a lake or pond — posited outside your property to the NNE, NE, and/or ENE is a great boon to you. When a body of water is situated in *any* of the other directions, it *enhances* negativity (yes, even when found in the auspicious sub-directions of the WNW and SSE) because in relationship to your property, the Water Element is not located in it's natural home, the NE. **Water anywhere in the NW** brings legal problems, great mental disturbances, and makes long-term success in your endeavors virtually impossible. **Water in the SW** is a life risk; it creates fear and disaster (by amplifying the 'incoming' negative energies height and weight protect against). **In the SE**, water is a dangerous defect, especially for women. It creates long-term health problems, depression, and conflicts in relationships, as well as fear and accidents. It is best to remember that the natural home of the Water Element is in the NE, whether on or near your property.

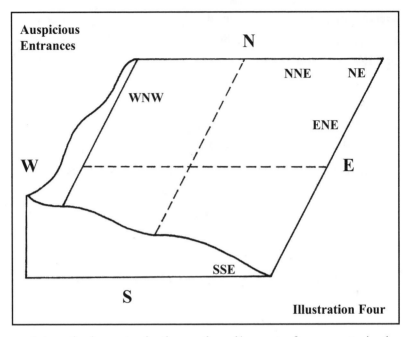

Illustration Four

Interestingly, water in the north and/or east of a property in the form of a stream or river may be another story. In this case, we must also consider its flow. When considering Movement — one of the four Main Principles of Vaastu — I said movement is best when it goes to the east or north. If a stream or river runs along or near the east side of your property but **the water flows south**, that's not good. Water in the east does bring clarity and good fortune, but when flowing south, it also brings anxiety, depression, illness, accidents, and financial problems. On the other hand, if it flows north, it brings success, fame, happiness, and tremendous prosperity.

Water in the north brings prosperity. But, if **the water flows to the west**, it brings mental problems, legal battles, defamation of character, and problems in relationships. When it flows to the east, it brings brilliant thoughts, happiness, good fortune (from every angle), and great prosperity.

The only exception to this rule of Water in the NE is when a nearby body of water is elevated, such as a mountain lake. If it's located to the west, SW, or south, it's fine energetically, as far as its location goes...*as long as you don't use it* recreationally. In effect, you can look but don't touch.

Additionally, as with a stream or river, how the water flows out of an elevated body of water is also important. If the elevated lake is located in the west and the stream flows down near your property, it should run along the northern border of your property and flow to the east. If it runs along the southern border of your property — even if it flows east — that's not good Vaastu. If the elevated lake is located in the south and the stream from it runs outside your property, for it to positively impact your property the stream must run along the east side (not the west) and flow north. Otherwise, it's a Vaastu defect and really not worth chancing.

A body of water on your property — whether manmade (such as a pool or fountain) or natural — is ideally placed in the NE quadrant. The one exception is if it is located in the center of the property. Water there brings happiness, but it will only last a generation or two, no longer.

Water *flowing* on your property is best when the *majority* of it is located on the northern or eastern side — regarding this point, we include the two northern quadrants (the NE and NW) and the two eastern quadrants (the NE and SE) — but **only if the majority of the water flows north and/or east**. In this way, you enhance the characteristics of the north (Abundance) and the east (Wisdom). Otherwise, the Water Element will enhance the negative qualities of the west side (the SW and NW) and/or those of the south side (the SW and SE). The same goes for the flow of water: if the water flows to the west and/or south, your life will crash. Since it's your property we're talking about, it's better to place the Water Element properly or fix it (or eliminate it) if it's not.

Size matters. An 'ill-situated' ocean, for example, can have almost incalculable negative effects simply because of its scale and proximity. But, these effects diminish dramatically with distance. If you live a mile or more from the ocean, the effects begin to diminish. Also, if you can't actually see the body of water, its effects are greatly diminished. But for them to be negligible you must be 50 miles away.

STRUCTURES AND THEIR TILT

If your property has an acceptable tilt (less than 20° off True North), then your **buildings ought to align with the property**. For example, if a property is square and tilts 13° off True North, your home — let's say it's also square or has a NE extension — should also have a 13° tilt off True North in the same direction, following the property line. Otherwise, it will cause adverse effects.

STRUCTURES AND THEIR SHAPE

I already mentioned that a four-sided rectangular shaped house/ building is excellent. The effects of this shape are enhanced if the building itself has a NE extension to it. If, however, you want *perfect* Vaastu in this regard, build or buy a circular home. The rules of Vaastu still apply regarding where you place the home on the property, but **in the case of a circular structure, no rules whatsoever apply for room placement**; it's all good. However, entrances/exits can *only* be located in the NE and/or SSE.

On the other hand, if you're going to buy or build an 'irregularly' shaped building — like a triangle, for example — you're setting yourself up for a great deal of difficulties. In such cases, the rules for auspicious and inauspicious cuts and extension are very important considerations. So, too, is movement and energy flow. For example, for an L-shaped house, you must build a partition wall between the two legs of the house, separating them *permanently*, with access between the two sections coming from outdoors. And, if you have a U-shaped home, the exterior open area 'inside' the 'U' must face either north or east, never south or west. It's a lot to consider. As you can see, simple is profoundly better.

INSIDE ACCESS

Just like property entrances/exits, all access to the house — and between interior spaces — should be from auspicious directions (NNE, NE, ENE, SSE, or WNW). Like that, doors and windows should also be aligned and auspiciously located. And, again, as much as possible, the majority of the movement indoors should also be in the direction of north and east.

THE ROOF OVER YOUR HEAD

Since every good Vaastu house or building shape should follow the Principles of Vaastu — such as greatest Height and Weight in the southwest, for example — the slant of the roof must also. An asymmetrical roof that extends primarily in a positive direction is more auspicious than a symmetrical one; so is a roof that slants *only* in a positive direction. However, most commonly, roofs are peaked. If the sides of the roof are balanced, at least one side will slant in a positive direction. If, however, they are asymmetrical, the longer side must slant downward in a positive direction. In any case, as long as the majority of the pitch of the roof is not in an inauspicious direction, you're fine. A flat roof is, of course, the exception.

WHEREFORE ART THOU?

Balanced balconies — to the north and south or east and west — are good Vaastu. A single balcony is best located in an auspicious direction — most preferably, in the N, NNE, ENE, or E. And, it's great Vaastu to have a corner balcony in the NE. But, never have connecting balconies in one auspicious direction and one inauspicious one. It creates an inauspicious extension and has very damaging effects.

GARAGES AND OTHER ATTACHMENTS

Garages are also best attached to the home in auspicious directions, since they extend the building shape wherever they are. Further, to make sure the extension is positive, butt the garage up to the corner of the building, aligned with the sides of the house. Otherwise, it will cause an inauspicious cut. If a garage is situated in an inauspicious sub-direction, ideally it should be free standing and not directly attached to the house (via an enclosed or roofed walkway, for example). This way, it is an entity unto itself. In any case, all garages must have auspicious entrances/exits. Lastly, if the garage is an interior garage — situated inside the home/building — it must also have an auspicious entrance/exit. Also, if it's located in the NE of the home, it should be kept clear of clutter as much as possible, following the Principle of Open Space.

The same Principles apply to porticos, raised attached decks, etc.

INSIDE THE HOME OF YOUR DREAMS

Where is the commanding position inside a property or home/building? The southwest. So, that's where the master bedroom should be located. Diagonally opposite, in the NE, the place of Abundance and Wisdom — where openness and peace are properly (and naturally) found — is the best location for a meditation room. An important side note: room(s) in the NE can have an attached shower and/or sink (the Water Element), but not a toilet (it's an Earth Element point, if you get my meaning).

Since the NW, the Home of the Air Element, offers mental clarity, dynamism, and spurs us to successful action, it's the best place for a home office or workspace. Also, if you don't want your children to zone out in front of the television or the computer, place their room in the NW. It's also a great place for a guest room or servant's quarters. If you have more than one floor in your home, the NW is a good place for a family room as well.

The SE, the home of the Fire Element, is the best location for a kitchen. Cooking should be done facing north or east, never south or west. Otherwise, you will 'cook' more than your food; you'll cook your family as well. The alternative for a well-placed kitchen (or fireplace) is the NW. Still, cooking should be done facing north or east, never south or west. *Within the kitchen,* fire is best placed in the SE or, as an alternative, in the NW of the room itself. If your kitchen is in the SW, it brings arguments and all sorts of conflicts into the home. When placed in the NE, a kitchen or fireplace will 'burn up' whatever money you make. It also creates illness, as well as arguments and conflicts.

MORE ON DREAMS

Where and how you sleep is important. In fact, it's one of the most important Vaastu points. Rest is the most prescribed non- prescription in health care, mental and physical. Without good sleep, your waking life will be a misery. It doesn't necessarily matter *how much* you sleep, but *how well.* Therefore, according to Vaastu, never...*ever*...sleep with your head facing north. That means the direction the top of your head 'faces' while you're lying prone can be any direction except north. **If you sleep with your head to the north, it's a real life risk.** You'll not only feel more irritable, frustrated, and emotionally unstable, you'll lose up to 50% of your willpower. And, no matter how much you meditate or do *sadhana*, your soul power will not increase while you sleep, which is part of the great spiritual value of the sleep state.

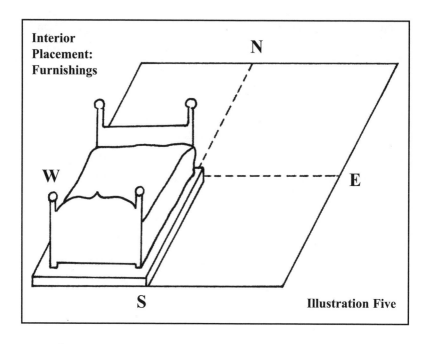

Interior Placement: Furnishings

N

W

E

S   **Illustration Five**

To increase your soul power and your good health, as well as feel more peaceful (and have good dreams), sleep with the top of your head facing south. For greater industriousness and increased longevity, face west. For greater health, more positive thoughts, and greater clarity, face east.

THE ART AND SCIENCE OF FURNITURE PLACEMENT

Again, think Height and Weight, Open Space, and Movement. Height and Weight belong in the SW. Open Space belongs in the NE. And, energy flow in any room is important. Ideally, your biggest and/or heaviest pieces are situated in the SW, getting lighter and/or lower as you move towards the north and east, with little or nothing in the NE corner. Furnishings are well placed along the walls, but not flat up against them. Of course, everything will extend out into the room. But, take that into consideration when designing your interiors. Ease of access is a valuable commodity.

DOWNWARD SLOPE — AN INTERIOR CONSIDERATION

How does Vaastu apply the Principle of Downward Slope to interior spaces? We mentioned this point earlier regarding stairs: when walking downward, we always land facing north or east. Yet its applications go even further. Wherever possible, rooms should be tiered downward to the north and east, and especially to the NE. This insures that where we 'land' — step down to — is in the direction of Abundance and/or Wisdom, leading us towards both. And, isn't that where we want to go in the present, as well as 'in the end'?

The subtlety of this point implies that within the comfort, peace, joy, and happiness of our favorite, most intimate environment, with each step we take we lay the groundwork for reaching our ultimate spiritual and material goals. In all these ways, your Vaastu adds to the presence of the Divine in your life, enhancing the moment...even quickening the pace...with each breath you take. And, isn't that the core intent and practicality of any spiritual science?

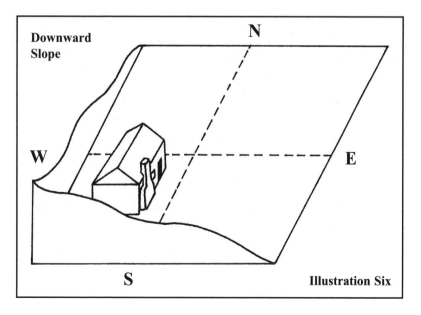

Downward Slope

N

W

E

S

Illustration Six

CHAPTER 7

THE MIDDLE WAY — HOW TO HAPPILY (AND QUICKLY) MAKE YOUR WAY ALONG THE RAZOR'S EDGE

In the ancient traditions, there are two 'general categories' of spiritual paths, which the Vedic tradition call *Aghora* and *Ghora*, sometimes deemed the Left and Right Hand of God, respectively. Ghora is presented as the 'sattvic' way — positive, peaceful, soothing, contemplative — a way to grow and nurture the seeds of Peace, Light, and Love, until you actually come to experience the profound breadth and depth of them. *Aghora* is presented, in many respects, as the flip-side: a fast-track march through the often terrifying shadow-worlds of 'negativity' — the flux of *rajas* and the dense and cloying *tamas* — through which one passes in a harrowing, break-neck race for the Divine Revelation and substantive, personal enlightenment. Robert Svoboda wrote some wonderful books on the path of the *Aghori*, the proponents of *Aghora*. But, something he said early on caught my eye — a point he made at the beginning of his first book on the subject. To begin the path, you must be fearless. I thought that was extremely cool. As more people I'd known — and others I'd come across — read these treatises, they began to chat about and offer their enthusiastic thumbs-up about it all. Yet, I was intrigued that, without exception, no one...not one... seemed to have picked up on this important, seemingly fundamental point.

It is said that some of the 'common' ingredients used in this path are intoxicants, as well as (many would say 'deviant') sexual practices, the consumption of dead and/or dying flesh (meat, in other words), and the use of 'unsavory' locations in which to do their 'work'

— in this case, their spiritual practices. Considering those points...enjoying intoxicants, sex, and eating meat, as well as the active pursuit of personal power...it could be argued that our Western lifestyle is a cultural example of a quasi-*Aghoric* path. To varying degrees, growing numbers of us plunge headlong into many such aspects of the 'negativity' — substance-abuse, sexual addictions, and fast-tracks to power (whatever we may deem that to be), etc. — but, certainly, not as a matter of fearlessness consciously guided towards spiritual fulfillment. In truth, we actively cultivate desire-driven laziness, fear-inspired escapism, and/or naïve ignorance — and, as often as not, these are nurtured by a rather biased socio-economic laissez-faire attitude. In other words, it's clearly more about desire, ignorance, and fear than fearlessness.

While the minority may be hell-bent for it, on the whole, we as a culture do indeed regularly seek whatever heightened moments we can temporarily experience — we seek the 'magic pill' — and, all with little if any understanding of the actual mechanics of the spiritual content of the processes we've set ourselves on; and, certainly, without much more thought or care for the possible/probable long-term 'side effects' of playing badly with fire, so to speak. What, in spiritual terms, is presented by its proponents as the fastest track to win enlightenment, in the hands of uninitiated, ignorant, predominantly materially-oriented 'aspirants' merely becomes a central expedient in creating more dysfunctional individuals, families, communities, and ultimately a dysfunctional culture. It's little wonder that those in the East, who have historical knowledge and experience on the subject and, for the most part, follow the *Ghoric* path anyway — have considered us, on the whole, 'infidels' and 'devil worshipers'. They see us playing with and nurturing the negativity without any real, substantive spiritual acumen at our disposal or imbued in our intent.

For the most part, in the West, those we consider 'on the spiritual path' have taken up the *Ghoric* Way as a sensible, spiritual alternative to our perennial, Western, quasi-*Aghoric* excesses. Peaceful environments, *sattvic* (vegetarian) diets, healthy/energy-enhancing physical regimens (*Hathayoga*, for example), stress-releasing forms of meditation and contemplation, practicing good behavior — kindness and selfless service towards others, compassion, saying only the 'sweet' truth, doing no harm — all play their part in nurturing this path. It may be said (if only whispered behind closed doors) that this is perhaps a more arduous path, since its divine results come to the aspirant more slowly. Still, for the majority of us, it seems the rational alternative to the 'debaucheries' of *Aghora*.

I've heard it argued that those following *Ghora* lack the courage to heartfully take up the path of *Aghora*. And, the response to this argument might rightly be that, in the end, fearlessness is a characteristic of the Enlightened, no matter how one gets there. So, why go through the muck and bother? But, even in this world of dualities, everything isn't just either black and/or white. There are shades of grey. At the heights of spirituality, there is a Middle Way, which includes the dash-and-dare component of the *Aghoric* path and the uplifting, 'positive' components of the Ghoric path. It is this third Way that is timely and most-suited to our present Age, being both thoroughly ancient and modern in its theory and practice. In this Way, we live mystically...now...not just in some glorious future, but today, in the here and now, without the need to wade deeper into the negativity or run from it in fear. It is not a 'magic' pill, like the ones you think you get from your local pharmacy. But, it is the real spiritual version — the miraculous tonic of Divine Wisdom. And, its side effects last forever.

Often, this term 'the Middle Way' is attached to the teaching propounded by the Buddha. It is said that he came upon it after searching and realizing the full extent of other paths — all of which fell under the 'categories' of *Aghora* or *Ghora*. But, I would argue that this is, at best, a misinterpretation. We each move along the path of our souls throughout each of our lives, lifetime after lifetime. Each stage, each twist and turn, is an important part of our singular path, a chapter in our personal story, the path of our soul. All the experiences that are recounted on the life of Siddhartha on his way to becoming the living form of the Buddha make up the warp and woof of his spiritual path in that incarnation. Each ingredient went into the recipe that culminated in the divine feast, which was his enlightenment. He was more than his teachings. He was a *living embodiment* of the Divine Wisdom — a truly shining, living, breathing, walking, talking, laughing, human example of the Divine, manifest in form on this plane, on this planet.

It is said that he won his enlightenment while faced with huge negativity — surrounded by demons, in fact, and confronted by the king of the demons, himself. It was in that moment, in his direct experience, that we see Siddhartha utterly fearless, at the same time at peace, and so divinely empowered with his own Self-effulgence that he vanquished the Darkness. It's not a stretch to say that that description, in itself, sounds pretty *Aghoric*. It is known that he went on to propound that his realization as the Buddha was the conquest of Nothingness over Something-ness — the peace of the Unbounded over the agitating flux of the Limited/Bound/Diminished/Duality. Doesn't that sound pretty *Ghoric* in tone?

I would propose that it makes little or no sense to conjecture that he summarily dropped all the wisdom and *shakti* (personal power) that he gained at each step of his spiritual sojourn and began again, *en toto*, right at the end. It seems more realistic…and more true to his divine, personal fragrance…to say that he actually built upon each of them, stage after stage, up to and beyond their culmination in his spiritual transformation from Siddhartha, the man, to the living Buddha, the conscious embodiment of the Divine. In truth, every divine soul passes through the same door — command over the fundamental forces in Nature. In our Tradition, this is called charging the Five Elements — the *panchabhutas,* the Pillars of Creation — to your soul. This is the nature of living mystically, of spiritual mastery. It is a process, a *sadhana.* Everything is made up of these Five Elements, which would include anything that falls under the heading of *Aghora* and/or *Ghora.* No matter what the details of the historical march, you will find, in every instance, bits and pieces of both Aghora and Ghora, no matter how substantive or miniscule one part or the other plays along the way. It is not required, nor particularly efficacious, to pursue wholly one at the exclusion of the other. What is important is that you win an intimate, soulful commanding on the fundamental forces of nature. And, remember, 'command' is not 'control'. It implies intimacy-by-agreement, a masterful harmony with the cosmic forces of the universe.

It is no small point to say that the Buddha also spoke to the need of his times, of the Age and conditions he found the world in, and to the tenor of the individual and collective consciousness of the people of his day. This is the nature of spiritual teachings. Students usually grasp only a small percentage of the Master's import. Their understanding is based on their personal soul capacity at the time and filtered through their personal blocks. It is a common thing that a Master's words are misinterpreted in his lifetime, and more so over time. It is only when spiritual Masters arise in greater and greater numbers that the fullness of the teachings can be more nearly understood and applied.

Students have shadowed their Masters since the dawn of human spirituality, but few reach the same heights or go beyond. Only a very few even reach the inner circle; that's been the common tradition, until now, the tenor of times past. However, it is in this Age that the real opportunity to substantively change the trend of time exists. That is our good fortune. Now, we can...and will...see a large number of true spiritual Masters walking this earth, enough to transform the *Kaliyuga*, this Age-in-transition of Ignorance and spiritual Darkness, into the spiritual fullness of the *Saiyuga*, the Age of Truth, Light, Peace, and Love.

In this new Age, with its inherent modern versions of the spiritual laws at play, we have the tremendous opportunity to ply the depths of the present 'new' world of spiritual awakening, while standing, as Newton said, on the shoulders of giants and becoming giants ourselves. Now, we can win our spiritual processes quickly, without ignoring the currents of negativity, nor diving into them. Thus, in our times, dash-and-dare *and* positivity, beauty, grace, kindness, and love go hand-in-hand.

We have the right and the duty to choose, in the ways that most inspire us personally, how to build our life — to choose the bricks and mortar of the temple of our own spirituality. But, no house or office or temple can stand long on anything but a firm foundation. Living in harmony with our environment, which the Vedic tradition thoroughly delineates in the science of Vaastu, is a vital part of that firm foundation. It plays a significant part in quickly winning our spiritual process. Its fundamentals are simple, yet have vast, far-reaching effects, which profoundly influence every single aspect, every single moment, of your life. It makes up 50% of your spiritual process. And, there is no compromising that, unless you simply wish to slow your progress down. Vaastu can change 80% of your karma, which you can prove to yourself and others from your own direct experience. Let's consider a few more points in this regard.

THE FLOW OF ENERGY AROUND YOU — ROADS AND ACCESS

Even within compound walls, you are not completely cut off from the energetics of the environment/world around you. They do structure and hold the integrity of your property, but they do not make it an insulated bubble. Energy also flows around your property. Some of this flow of energy — and the positive or negative influence it conveys — is created by roads, which provide access to or run alongside your property. Since we are talking both theory and practical application here, the more roads the merrier. If an ideal property shape is rectangular, then four roads bordering the property would also be considered ideal.

As mentioned earlier, optimal access to the property (via gates and driveways) should ideally occur in the northeast quadrant from the auspicious sub-divisions — from the NNE and/or the ENE. This would imply that optimal/auspicious access would come by having roads along the north and east boundaries of the property. But, as you now know, there are other auspicious entrances/exits possible, from the SSE and the WNW also. If roads bound the property only from these two sides — along the south and/or west of the property — they do offer auspicious access, yes, though not the 'most' auspicious. However, they are viable options. And, there are others.

Auspicious entrances/exits placed directly opposite each other also add to their auspiciousness — a WNW entrance/exit *and* an ENE one...or a NNE entrance/exit *and* a SSE one. Other combinations — such as SSE and ENE accesses, for example — are not as good as the ones just mentioned above, but they are good; that is to say, in effect, they are auspicious, just not as auspicious. It is better to have entrances/exits directly across from each other. Whenever we have the opportunity to have the best, we should shoot for that.

Roads not only offer access to our property, but provide a flow of energy around it as well, which can support and balance the energetics of the property itself or act to diminish them, even 'attack' them. A road that 'hits' your property — runs directly into it — is considered a Vaastu defect, unless it hits in an auspicious direction. Roads draw the surrounding community to you and you to the community. Therefore, they also present that exchange of energy — whether negative or positive — as an influence in your life.

Additionally, since directional strength is a key ingredient in Vaastu, how we actually move out into the community impacts our relationship with it, as well. Remember, Vaastu is everywhere. Our community also has its own intrinsic Vaastu. Therefore, when moving out into the community, it is most auspicious to travel in auspicious directions. So, for example, if your home is situated in or to the southwest of your town, you automatically have a commanding position/energetic on the community. Traveling along auspicious routes to work — driving north and/or east — add to that commanding and auspicious energy. Ideally, we don't want to travel south to reach our workplace, to step out into the world. Like that, if we live to the northwest of town or the southeast, we have a kind of equitable balance between our selves and the community in the command department. However, if we live to the northeast, the community commands on us. And, considering the state of 'material' affairs in the world as it has been — 75% negative and 25% positive — that energetic can be highly debilitating to us. If you look closely, you will find that those living in that position have a strong tendency towards dysfunctional behavior and, often, great material/financial flux. If you find yourself in such a circumstance, change it. Change your Vaastu and you change your life.

A VISION OF FUTURE POSSIBILITIES

What if the community around/next to you was also built with good Vaastu? How strongly might the roads — the connecting energetics — positively enhance your property and your life? At my Master's ashram in Penukonda (the word ashram itself means 'community'), each area is conscribed by compound walls; in effect, each sections holds its own integrity and positive energy, while influencing the other sections at the same time. There is a road along the far side of the eastern wall of the main area — the area which houses the temple (to Shirdi Sai Baba and Jesus) in the southwest, as well as a second temple/sacred power spot (known as the Dwarkamai) nearby, both of which look out onto the open expanse of the gardens. Again, all these are within the same section. This road running N/S along the E-side of that section directly hits the SE apartments of the student-housing complex, making a very auspicious NNE entrance/exit to it. Because of this, the inhabitants of these apartments get a huge flow of the positive energetics of Abundance from the north, which was the point in constructing it that way. Good Vaastu can produce extraordinary results.

TRUE CREATIVE ARTISTRY

Some may think the thorough application of the guidelines of Vaastu extend so far as to stifle one's artistic, architectural, or design creativity. No way. Definitely, Vaastu's guidelines impact every minute aspect of the make-up of your environment (inside and out), but they in no way diminish the virtually infinite possibilities for *positive* creative expression. This word 'positive' is not an arbitrary adjective here; it's a pointed one. Good Vaastu is about enhancing and supporting the structure and flow of Nature's positive energies, which are in a very practical sense infinite. However, if your creativity necessarily extends to every negative possibility as well, then yes there's no denying it, good Vaastu will thwart your efforts. In such a case, first…you might as well put down this book. Secondly, go out and buy or own or rent any place you wish (you can do this with your eyes closed). There are plenty of options already in place…pretty much any place you go…that would fit this bill. However, if real creativity is an actual desire or necessity in your life, then you can and will see/experience the infinite growth and expression of creativity *in every aspect of your life* by buying or owning or renting even a small hut, if it's built according to Vaastu. With Vaastu's help, you step into the true realm of creative expression, both spiritual and material.

The techniques for artistry may have changed over time according to the medium one works in. Yet, the fundamentals remain. When your canvas is your life, the fundamentals most certainly apply: you are in relationship with your environment, with other souls, and you are moving through some incarnation along the path of your personal, spiritual unfoldment. And, as the artist of your life, your perception in the present greatly impacts all three through the art of personal expression.

How we participate and express ourselves is a reflection of our soul capacity. Which brings us back to dash-and-dare. This is one of the most beautiful characteristics (seen again and again) in the lives of great souls. Since the present forms of the spiritual laws dictate that even in the midst of huge obstacles or negative energies we can win great material wealth and abundance and true, divine success in our spiritual endeavors, it behooves us to master them. Developing the art of dash-and-dare is a true asset in this regard.

THE ART OF DASH & DARE

Everything that occurs — the machinations of our material circumstances as well as the movement along the path of our soul and 'its' enlightenment — is, after all, the Divine Play. It's a play. My Master often says it's of great value to take life 'sporty', in a playful and sporting manner. At a recent gathering of hundreds of students he mentioned how he recognized their suffering and the miseries they often found themselves embroiled in. But, he also spoke of the silliness of this perspective. He asked the group to consider the perspective that life...all of it...is a gift from God and that it is, in fact, our attachments and our personal blocks that hinder us from recognizing and living this higher, more 'realistic' truth. It is a fundamental characteristic of dash-and-dare to accept what comes in a sporty way, accepting whatever does come open-heartedly, while maintaining our clarity of mind, holding our personal power (our *shakti*) at the ready, ever-seeing the miraculous possibilities (if not the outward symptoms) of the moment, and remaining open to the opportunity for a quantum leap in our personal experience...now.

If you think about it, dash-and-dare is the underlying thread, perhaps even the practical essence, of all substantive Self-Help regimens, which apply to business, interpersonal relationships, and all aspects and stages of our gaining real success in our daily lives, in our own personal 'play'. So, how do we do this, practically speaking, in our lives? Regarding Vaastu, it's easy to see that, for example, your taste in home furnishings won't compromise your Vaastu; in Vaastu, it's more about placement than about whether it's an armoire from Southern France or IKEA®. And, it doesn't matter if your house is a Spanish style hacienda or an English Tudor townhouse. Curtains or shades are of no consequence, as long as the window they highlight is auspiciously placed and they're open to allow the dawn's healing light into your home. What things you put in your home are simply for your delight. It's all part of the play. The only thing to be wary of is that the rooms in your home or office don't become 'gluzzy' — cluttered or filled with too many old or worn-out things. But, luckily, that's why God invented the garage sale and Goodwill®.

But, of course, dash-and-dare extends much farther than interior architectural design and home furnishings. The real 'interior design' applications have to do with further enhancing your conscious connection with your soul. My Master, for example, is known for his dash-and-dare. Most examples have to do with his own spiritual processes, which he relates freely, both his successes and his failures. Besides the qualities of courage/fearlessness, acceptance, and playfulness, dash-and-dare implies readiness, clarity of thought and purpose, and a willingness to fulfill your commitment to whatever it is you're engaged in.

In spirituality, this also means forging a personal willingness to seize the possibilities of the moment while holding your personal power, under whatever circumstances you find yourself in. The story of Tenali Ramakrishna, which I related earlier, is a case in point. When standing face-to-face with the huge divine energy and presence of Mother Divine, herself (in the form of *MahaKali*), he was offered a boon with two distinct 'options' — she held out 2 bowls, one containing milk and the other curd/yoghurt — one energetically offering the fullness of wisdom and the other the fullness of abundant material wealth. She said he could have whichever one he wished. He paused a moment, then asked to take a sip from each, to see which one he liked best. So, she handed him both bowls. At that, he poured the contents of one bowl into the other. Raising the bowl with the mixture in it and said, "I'll take this one." She smiled and gave her blessing. Soon after, he became a favored teacher, friend, and high counselor in the court of King Krishnadevaraya. He had the presence of mind (and, some would say, the temerity) to mix the two together and, in so doing, won both. This is dash-and-dare.

You might consider that, from our side, we don't know whether this is our last day or not. Making the best of it seems a wholly brilliant thing to do. If you lived today as if it was your last, what would that be like? I'm not talking about some fantasy last day, where you'd go to Tahiti or something. No, I'm referring to *this* day, part of which you're spending reading this book. If we pretend that it's your good fortune to live out this day, fall asleep, and breathe your last breath, how would you spend this day? If you really owned this thought, you might find that you'd quickly get beyond regrets, fear, and anger and decide it would be more worthwhile to spend your last waking hours filled with peace and gratitude and expressing them — and open to whatever opportunities for more Truth, Light, Peace, and Love that might arise. How bad a day would that be? Since it's a 'real' day, you'd still get up, go to work, see some folks — whatever the day had in store — but, *you* would be different...kinder, more compassionate, and forgiving...and happier, as well as ready and more willing to participate *well* in whatever comes your way. And, if it was God's will, and you woke up again...today...once again owning that this is your last day, how would you live it — this, your last day? Truly consider this: how do you think this kinder, more compassionate, peaceful you would impact the very real possibility of winning your enlightenment in *this* moment, during this breath?

And, how much more powerful and fulfilling would this day be if you lived it breathing in the rarified air of a truly sacred place...your own home? How far-fetched is it to think that one of the saints that walked the hallowed ground within your own compound walls was you? It's not a stretch at all. And it's truly up to you.

We live in a time of rediscovery. While in the coming days scientific thought will certainly still make advances, the real depth of knowledge to be fully grasped is nor new but ancient. And, truly, this knowledge now revealed is meant to...and will...change the trends of time. As more of the ancient wisdom comes to light, it will be evident to all that the veil of Man's ignorance of the Divine is being lifted, that our way has always been mapped out for us, our progress always assured. Although we may have perceived our search as a meandering through the Ages of the past, still we have come to this point in the history of our illumination: now, at the turn of the Age, after treading the path of our souls from incarnation to incarnation we stand at the doorway to the treasury of the Infinite. It is time for us as a community to knock and, through God's grace, enter.

Divine is divine — it's not a matter of religion or cultural background. Since the dawn of time, the community of saints has gathered to share its wisdom and experience and to preserve the wealth of its teachings and practices for coming generations; by reincarnating again and again specifically for that purpose and by passing on its knowledge to the few who had the capacity to embody it, they have added to its wealth. Now, as a result of their good woerks...and ours...the floodgates are opening. And so, in keeping with this holy tradition, it is our present task to come together at this truly auspicious time in the history of mankind to drink in the divine knowledge as deeply and as fully as we can, to recount the spiritual experiences we've had along the path of our souls, to share the wonderful, illuminating stories of those who have tread this divine path before us, and to know that it is time...through God's grace...for us to walk in their footsteps.

In this most ancient and modern way, we shall create something new. By manifesting the power of the sacred wisdom in ourselves, we manifest it in the world around us to such an extent that through our collective soul power we shall realize the fruition of our deepest longings: a powerful, sacred world where anything...every divine thing...is possible.

GLOSSARY

ABHISHEK. Bathing the temple icon — the water is charged with miraculous, healing energy and given to worshipers.

ADISHANKARA. A great saint, the reviver of the Vedic tradition subsequent to the coming of the Buddha, and founder of the Swami order in India.

AKASHA. Infinite space — one of the 5 Elements — which in Kaleshwaravaastu® is called 'Sky'.

AHAM BRAHMASMI. "I am everything/everything is Me".

AMRUTA. The divine immortal nectar.

ATMALINGAM. An 'egg-shaped stone' created/birthed by a saint, which carries his/her soul power.

AVATARA. A fully conscious incarnation of the Divine.

AYURVEDA. The Vedic system of natural (nature-based) healthcare.

BENARES. A holy city in India, beloved of Shiva (also known as Varanasi and Kashi).

BHARATA. An ancient name for India.

BIJAKSHARAS. Sacred sounds.

BRAHMAN. The Source, Course, and Goal of all; the Nameless-and-the-Named; the Unbounded Absolute Oneness; That, of which every thing IS.

DAKSHINA. 'Donation'…also, 'displaying auspiciousness'. It's also a name for an aspect of Mother Divine, which means 'the way to approach'. Associated with Durga (which means 'Unapproachable'), 'Dakshina', therefore, is also the way to approach the Unapproachable (the Divine) — connoting one's fitness for receiving Divine blessings.

DARSHAN. Seeing the Divine with your own two eyes.

DECLINATION. The angular difference between True North and Magnetic North.

DHUNI. A saint's fire pit.

DIKSHAS. The guidelines for spiritual practices.

DIVINE LINEAGE. The illustrious, direct line of spiritual masters, which dates back to the primordial guru, Dattatreya, and includes Shirdi Sai Baba, Jesus, Ramana Maharshi, Ramakrishna Paramahamsa, and Sri Sai Kaleshwara.

DWARKAMAI. A dilapidated masjid in the village of Shirdi, which was the home of Shirdi Sai Baba. Also, a building at Sri Sai Kaleshwara's ashram in Penukonda, which will eventually house his mahasamadhi shrine.

FENG SHUI. The Chinese ('grandson') version of Vaastu.

FOUR VEDIC AGES. Satyuga, Tretayuga, Dwarapayuga, and our present

Kaliyuga.

GHORA AND AGHORA. The two 'general categories' of spiritual paths in the Vedic tradition — sometimes deemed the Right and Left Hand of God, respectively — Ghora being the positive, gentle, seemingly slow path, while Aghora is considered a dangerous albeit fast-tracked path.

GUNAS. Sattva (pure), Rajas (agitation), Tamas (inertia).

HAFIZ. A Sufi saint known for his exquisite poetry, which recounted his personal experiences with the Divine, his Beloved.

HUNDHI. Holds the dakshina. For example, the offerings bin/box (for donations) at a temple.

JAPA. Mental repetition of sacred formulas (with eyes open or closed) used to charge them to one's soul, to build one's personal shakti, and to increase one's soul capacity.

JESUS. A spiritual master of the Divine Lineage, known to have studied and won many of his spiritual processes in India. He is considered the most unique, powerful divine soul in the universe.

JYOTISH. Vedic astrology, the 'Science of Light', which gives an accurate portrait of the path of one's soul.

KALA (also MahaKala). The Lord of Time, a name of Shiva.

KALIYUGA. The Dark Age — our present Age — when negativity dominates; where the energy is 75% negative and 25% positive.

KARMA. The reaction to the actions you've created through the illusion that is covering you.

KRISHNADEVARAYA. The saint-king of Southern India — who ruled over 400 hundred years ago — he lived in the ancient sacred power spots of Hampi and Penukonda, and built hundreds of temples, including the Golden Temple at Tirupati.

LEELA. Play (or game), illusion (or testing), which comes from one of 3 directions: nature/Mother Divine, the master/the line of masters, or your self.

LORD KRISHNA. An avatara of MahaVishnu.

LORD RAMA. An avatara of MahaVishnu.

LORD VENKATESHWARA. The avatara of MahaVishnu for the present Age, who resides in the Golden Temple complex in the town of Tirupati as a living, 'stone statue'.

MAHARISHIS. Literally, 'Great Seers'. Men and women of extraordinary insight and miraculous spiritual power, who cognized the many aspects of the Divine and researched the effects, both as they relate to individual and collective consciousness and to nature.

MAHASAMADHI. When a divine soul 'drops his body'.

MAHESHWARA. Literally, 'Great Lord' — another name for Shiva.

MANTRA. Sacred formulas used during spiritual practices, consisting of bijaksharas, which open specific energetic channels to the Divine.

MAYA. The grand illusion of life-and-death, the force behind the 'substance' of appearances, and our attachment to it.

MURTI. The holy icon/image in a temple or on an altar.

PANCHABHUTAS. The fundamental Elements of nature, the 5 Vedic 'pillars of creation': earth, fire, sky (akasha), water, and air.

POORNAAVATARA. 100% incarnation in human form of an aspect of the Divine, such as Mother Divine (MahaKali).

PRANA. 'Life force' or breath.

PRASAD. A gift/blessing from the Divine.

PURANAS. The 'Old Stories' (histories) in the Vedic scriptures.

RAMAKRISHNA PARAMAHAMSA (1836 - 1886). A spiritual master of the Divine Lineage, known for his huge devotion to Mother Divine in the form of MahaKali.

RAMANA MAHARSHI (1879 - 1950). A spiritual master of the Divine Lineage, who lived most of his life on or near Arunachala, a sacred mountain beloved of Shiva by the village of Tiruvannamalai.

SADHANA. Spiritual practices.

SAIYUGA. The Illumined Age, which will last 1,000 years. We are at the commencement of the Age of Sai.

SANSKRIT. One of the oldest languages known to man, its alphabet consists of bijaksharas (sacred sounds), which are the vibratory components of most of the spiritual practices from India.

SAPTARISHIS. The seven 'original' Great Seers of the Vedic civilization.

SATCHITANANDA. Absolute bliss consciousness, the 'fragrance/direct experience' of Brahman.

SHAKTI. Spiritual power/force. Also, a name of Mother Divine.

SHIVA. In Creation, he is the Divine Masculine, the Auspicious One, the Commander of the 5 Elements. Also, one of the Divine Trinity along with Brahma (the Creator) and MahaVishnu (the Maintainer/Operator).

SHIRDI SAI BABA (1840 - 1918). One of India's most-beloved saints, who lived as a beggar in the small Indian village of Shirdi for over 40 years, during which time he performed thousands of miracles and healings, gaining hundreds of thousands of devotees (now, millions). In 1987, he appeared in physical form before the 14-year-old Kaleshwar and re-awakened his divine powers and knowledge.

SHIVALINGAM. An 'egg-shaped' stone, which is associated with the power of Shiva.

SHRADDHA AND SABURI. 'Faith and patience', a favorite saying of Shirdi Sai Baba; literal translation in Telugu/Sanskrit is also 'devoted/constant attention and disciplined practice'.

SHRUTI AND SHMRITI. Divinely revealed (directly cognized)

knowledge and knowledge gained by observation of practical applications in nature.

SRI AUROBINDO (1872 - 1950). A prolific author and poet, freedom fighter for India's independence, evolutionary philosopher and teacher, who took up the path of spirituality while a young man, spending much of the rest of his life as a recluse, writing spiritual treatises from his ashram located in the town of Pondicherry on India's East coast.

SRI SAI KALESHWARA (1973 -). A poornaavatara, a living spiritual master in the Divine Lineage of Shirdi Sai Baba, Jesus, Ramakrishna Paramahamsa, and Ramana Maharshi. His mission in this incarnation is to make spiritual masters, not just spiritual students. Soul friend/brother, and spiritual master of the author. His ashram — a natural and super-natural/spiritual paradise built according to Vaastu — is located in Penukonda, Andhra Pradesh, India.

SRI SAILAM. Home of a magnificent Shiva temple, which houses a powerful 'stone' (shivalingam) of super-natural origin.

VAASTU. A part of the Vedic sciences of ancient India, which deals specifically with the influences of the cosmic forces in nature on the quality of life of the inhabitants of a particular place. It was the first 'natural' science of architecture, pre-dating Feng Shui by more than 3,000 years. Vaastu is 50% of spirituality.

VISHVAMITRA. The great and ancient sage who cognized the Gayatri mantra, said to be equal to all the Vedas.

YAGYAM. Vedic ritual/ceremony, using the transformational energy of fire (the Fire Element) to produce the desired effects.

YANTRA. Soul diagram/symbol — the hidden home of one's soul energy.

YOGAVASISTHA. The written record of an enlightening conversation between Guru Vasistha (Lord Rama's family guru) and his divine student.

O books

O is a symbol of the world, of oneness and unity. In certain cultures it also means the "eye", symbolising knowledge and insight, and in Old English it means "place of love or home". O Books explore the many paths of wholeness and understanding which different traditions have developed through the ages.

In philosophy, metaphysics and aesthetics O represents zero relating to immensity, indivisibility and fate. This list challenges systems and assumptions where "nothing" is absent but substance is still missing.

For more information on the full list of over 300 titles please visit our website **www.O-books.net**

myspiritradio is an exciting web, internet, podcast and mobile phone global broadcast network for all those interested in teaching and learning in the fields of body, mind, spirit and self development. Listeners can hear the show online via computer or mobile phone, and even download their favourite shows to listen to on MP3 players whilst driving, working, or relaxing.

Feed your mind, change your life with O Books,
The O Books radio programme carries interviews with most authors, sharing their wisdom on life, the universe and everything...e mail questions and co-create the show with O Books and myspiritradio.

Just visit **www.myspiritradio.com** for more information.

The Feng Shui Diaries
Richard Ashworth

The daily work of one of Britain's very few feng shui men: touching, informative, and very funny.

1846940176 200pp **£9.99 $16.95**

The House of Wisdom
Yoga of the East and West

Swami Maharaj and Santoshan

Focuses on the spiritual path of yoga, encouraging spiritual growth along with creative and skilful living. This penetrates the heart of spiritual wisdom. It is destined to become an important classic. **Glyn Edwards**, Arthur Findlay College

1846940249 240pp **£11.99 $22.95**

The Book of One
The spiritual path of Advaita

Dennis Waite

3rd printing

A magisterial survey that belongs on the shelves of any serious student.
Scientific and Medical Network Review

1903816416 288pp **£9.99 $17.95**

Everything is a Blessing
Make your life a little easier, less stressful and more meaningful
David Vennells

I've read a few self-help books in my time, but this is the only one I've ever talked about with no reserve or irony. Vennells charmed me utterly with his open enthusiasm, simple presentations of deep spiritual truths, suggestions for achievable goals and workable plans and doable exercises. **Marion Allan Reviews**
1905047223 160pp £11.99 $19.95

How to Meet Yourself
...and find true happiness
Dennis Waite

A comprehensive survey of the psychological and philosophical dynamics of the human condition, offering an everlasting solution to discovering true happiness in the moment. I highly recommend it. Dennis Waite is one of the foremost contemporary writers on Advaita Vedanta in the West. **Paula Marvelly**, author of *The Teachers of One*.
1846940419 260pp £11.99 $24.95

The Jain Path: Ancient Wisdom for the West
Aidan Rankin

The best introduction to Jainism available. It is at once very topical, clear and engaging. David Frawley (Pandit Vamdeva Shastri), Director of the American Institute of Vedic Studies. A book that is full of wisdom and intelligence. **William Bloom**, Director of The Holism Network
1905047215 240pp **£11.99 $22.95**